PENGUIN BOOKS

MEMOIRS OF A BEATNIK

Diane di Prima was born in Brooklyn, New York, in 1934. She began writing at the age of seven, and committed herself to the life of poetry at the age of fourteen. In 1953 she left college and moved to Manhattan, where she lived and wrote for many years. During this period she met and worked with such writers as Jack Kerouac, Allen Ginsberg, and LeRoi Jones (Amiri Baraka). She founded Poets Press and the New York Poets Theatre, and became known as an important writer of the Beat movement.

For the past thirty years she has lived and worked in northern California. She is the author of thirty-two books of poetry and prose. Her most recent book is an expanded version of her epic poem *Loba* (Penguin). Her memoir *Recollections of My Life as a Woman* will be published by Viking in 1999.

Memoirs of a Beatnik

Diane di Prima

PENGUIN BOOKS

PENGUIN BOOKS
Published by the Penguin Group
Penguin Putnam Inc., 375 Hudson Street,
New York, New York 10014, U.S.A.
Penguin Books Ltd, 27 Wrights Lane,
London W8 5TZ, England
Penguin Books Australia Ltd, Ringwood,
Victoria, Australia
Penguin Books Canada Ltd, 10 Alcorn Avenue,
Toronto, Ontario, Canada M4V 3B2
Penguin Books (N.Z.) Ltd, 182–190 Wairau Road,
Auckland 10, New Zealand
Penguin India, 210 Chiranjiv Tower, 43 Nehru Place,
New Delhi 11009, India

Penguin Books Ltd, Registered Offices:
Harmondsworth, Middlesex, England

First published in the United States of America by Olympia 1969
Published by The Last Gasp of San Francisco 1988
Published in Penguin Books 1998

10 9 8 7 6 5

Copyright © Diane di Prima, 1969, 1988
All rights reserved

ISBN 0 14 02.3539 6
(CIP data available)

Printed in the United States of America
Set in Galliard

Author's Note

"What do you suppose happened to all those Beatniks?" mused a blonde freshman as she drove me back to San Francisco after my reading at Berkeley last year.

Well sweetie, some of us sold out and became hippies. And some of us managed to preserve our integrity by accepting government grants, or writing pornographic novels. John Wieners is mad and in make-up in Buffalo, Fred Herko walked out a window, Gary Snyder is a Zen priest. You name it. Or, as my eleven-year-old daughter recently said to me, remembering the early years of her childhood:

"I really miss those old days. They were hard, but they were beautiful."

Things now are more like pretty. A New Age, with a bit of the baby fat still showing.

Stay stoned.

Diane di Prima
May 1969

Memoirs of a Beatnik

Chapter 1—February

I awoke to the sounds of morning in the West Village. The sounds of traffic. Trucks were going by outside and the pavement was wet. They were nervous, honking and snorting at one another. The window was open and the shade was flapping a little, one side of it hitting the window frame over and over in an irregular rhythm. I opened my eyes, turned over in bed and looked at my surroundings.

The room was a bright yellow, which offset the pale grey light of the rainy dawn. Aside from our low bed, the only furniture in the room was made of skids stolen from nearby paper companies and painted a flat black. They served as both chairs and tables, and no cushions broke the austerity of the furnishings, no draped Indian prints and antique velours such as we have become accustomed to in the sixties. One large platform, placed against the wall which faced the foot of the bed, held a candle at least a foot in diameter and about three and a half feet high. Ivan was particularly proud of this candle. He had pointed it out to me when we first got to his place, saying that it had taken

3

seventeen dollars worth of wax to make it. It had been our light during the night's proceedings.

Although we were only on the second floor, the room had been "decorated" with some kind of false eaves. They sloped slightly over the windows and enclosed the bed in shadow. It was a large room, and the newness of the paint job and the flawlessly finished floor made it seem like a rather affluent garret. As if the folk in *La Bohème* had come into some money and painted everything, I thought with a grin.

Through an archway I could just get a glimpse of the closet-sized kitchen, shining with new utensils. To the right of the kitchen, I knew, there was an equally tiny bathroom, flawlessly tiled and equipped with deep-napped, fluffy towels in dark luxurious colors and a variety of expensive bath oils. A perfect miniature, a doll house; and somebody was playing house here, sure enough.

Well, here I was. I stretched my legs, arching my toes and sighing just a little, so as not to waken the boy still sleeping beside me. Here I was and, I thought wryly, this is only the first of many strange apartments I'll be waking up in. The muscles of my thighs felt sore, and I passed my hand over them to feel the graininess of the dried come that was stuck to them here and there. Then I slid my hand between my legs and felt softly of the lips of my vagina. The skin was raw as I slipped my fingers inside, exploring gently. He certainly was a big one, I thought. A big one for the first one, that was good. A shiver of pleasure passed over me as I explored the familiar ground and goose bumps started up on my arms. Now, I thought with a little grin of cynical

4

pleasure, I certainly won't have any more trouble using Tampax.

Ivan was still asleep, his back to me. I softly slid the sheet off both of us, and compared the rosy, almost violet cast of my flesh with the pallid, olive light that his body threw off. We looked good together. It was a pleasure to lie there, mildly aroused, passing my hand over the smooth skin of my own breasts and stomach, and knowing that at any moment I could initiate the dance that would satisfy my own desire and bring delight to the creature beside me.

I turned on my side and put my mouth on his back, lightly tonguing the indent his spine made. He had one large vertebra there at his lower back, just before his spine curved in between the cheeks of his ass. I explored it thoroughly with my mouth, traced the spine to its end, and started up again, this time bringing my fingers into play, brushing them lightly over his flanks and sides, raising the fine down that covered his sallow skin.

Ivan was thoroughly awake by now, stirring beneath my touch, and as I raked the hair on the nape of his neck with my tongue, he turned toward me, covering my mouth with his own. I slid my arm under his shoulders, noticing as I did so that for all his length his shoulders were very slight—as slight as a girl's. For some reason this excited me all the more, and I moved my body so that I half lay on him, and devoted my full attention to our kiss.

There are as many kinds of kisses as there are people on the earth, as there are permutations and combinations of those people. No two people kiss alike—no two people fuck alike—but somehow the kiss is even more personal, more individualized than the fuck.

There are those who kiss intently, earnestly, their lips tight and straining, their tongues hard, thrust with a firm determination as far as possible into the other's mouth; there are those who kiss lackadaisically, casually, languorously, their mouths slack, brushing lightly, their tongues almost unequal to the effort of venturing forth. There are those cunning kissers whose kiss seems casual at first, and sneaks up on you in vast explosions of lust. There are those insinuating kissers whose kiss is so lewd that it leaves you slightly repelled, as if you had just had a quick fuck on the bathroom floor; and those virginal kissers who, in the act of turning your mouth practically inside out, seem chastely to be taking your hand. There are those who kiss as if they were fucking: tongue pumping frantically back and forth between the other's lips in a breathless rhythm. There are many, many other major types of kisses—at least twelve come to my mind offhand. List your favorites below:

Our kiss began at the lips, mouth loose, relaxed, playing and brushing each other gently, seeking to blend into each other, to become one mouth, but with no urgency about it. The excitement built gradually, until lips were being ground savagely against the still-closed teeth. A slacking off, and then his tongue came out and began to examine the inside of my lower lip, prodding and sliding gently into the corners, rubbing against my gums and curving my lip down. The tongue withdrew, and mine moved to follow suit, to play the same game but more thoroughly, slipping around the inside of the upper lip also, and down into the sides of his mouth, puffing out first one of his hollow cheeks and then the other. When I tired of this, I fell to nipping the inside of his lower lip with my teeth. And then his tongue reached out again, serious and straining, searching out the roof of my mouth, and the skin under my tongue. We shifted in order to lock mouths and bodies more closely together, and my hand found his large, beautiful cock and began to stroke it and fondle it, occasionally pausing to cup its full knob in the hollow of my palm.

Our tongues were jousting now in a fine fencing match of pleasure, touching and tilting as we moved slightly from side to side in our attempts to bring our flesh into more and more total contact. I slid a knee up under his balls and rotated it gently, while examining his entire palate with the tip of my tongue. In reply, he pressed one thigh awkwardly against my crotch, just touching my clitoris. A warm wave of pleasure spread over me, and I began to grind my box against his leg, gripping him with both my thighs, while my mouth left his and sought the hollow place I loved at the base of his throat.

He lay there, his head thrown back and his eyes closed, as I traced the line of his throat, his collarbone and his breast with my mouth, leaving a fine trail of saliva on his pale skin. My tongue played briefly with his hard, slight nipples, and I continued my journey south, pausing now and then to nip the fine, smooth flesh just under his ribs, or to ream his navel with my tongue. His eager hands on my head now thrust me down, down toward his huge cock, but I resisted, playfully. I was not to be hurried. I took one of the dark hairs on his stomach between my front teeth and pulled at it lightly. I traced the fine bones of his pelvis with my mouth, studying the way the flesh, stretched taut, dipped into a hollow, smooth and sensuous as sand dunes. I left a purple tooth mark there and went slowly on my way. Ivan groaned once. His hands, letting up slightly on their pressure, began to play frantically in my hair. I mouthed and tongued the smooth skin between his navel and groin, until the muscles leaped and twitched under my touch and I could hear his quick, involuntary gasps.

I slid my body down along his leg, until my mouth found his standing cock. I began to play with it, nibbling along its sides with my lips, tonguing here and there at its root, in the tangle of dark, musty-smelling hair. At last, under the urgent message of his hands, my mouth closed over the large head of his cock, and I tasted the bittersweet liquid at its tip. I bent my head down as far as I could, completely filling my mouth, straining to make that space larger and to take him in more completely. The head of his cock pressed against the back of my throat and I gagged slightly, but his mounting excitement drove all other thought from my mind. I slid my hands under his buttocks, and drew him closer to me, moving my head up and down, and pressing my own wet opening tight against his knee. My head was swimming; my blurred sight registered a patch of sunlight on the yellow wall over and over again. I remember thinking irrelevantly that the rain had stopped. I could hear Ivan gasping and moaning above me.

My own desire became more urgent. I wanted that large pulsing cock inside of me. I withdrew my mouth from it swiftly as a shudder ran through him. I paused briefly to tongue his full, round balls and, sliding my body up over his, I raised myself with my arms and straddled him so that my moist hole was just above his rod. I lowered myself onto it, guiding it to the proper place, and squirming down over it to take it into my still tight opening. But there was more. I had not taken the huge tool in fully. We separated slightly and I slid one leg up, over his shoulder. His hands on my backside drew me close and closer—he was in, up to the hilt. My body seemed to be melting, a grey mist spilled before my eyes. We lay on our sides, one of my legs stretched out under me and one over his shoulder. We pumped and circled in a mounting tide of ecstasy. My long hair had come loose and cascaded over us both. At last I gave way, my entire body filled with pleasure, and felt the flood of delight sweep through my flesh as his warm come filled my cunt to overflowing, and with a shuddering shout he collapsed on top of me.

I know that it was a long time before we moved, because when I raised my head I saw that the patch of yellow sunlight had moved quite some distance across the wall, and sunk down somewhere near the woodwork. I moved my leg a little, and Ivan slid his limp wet cock out of me, causing an exquisite and delicate sensation. He reached across me with one arm and picked up the electric

9

alarm clock which had been knocked over by our exertions. Gave a long whistle when he saw the time, started to pry himself loose, then fell to kissing my eyelids and tugging at my ear with his lips. I slid over to a drier place on the sheet. He pulled a loose strand of my hair across my face, spreading it like a web, and kissed me through it. Our tongues met as if through a veil. I said, "Umph."

"Hungry?" he asked, sitting up and swinging his legs over the side of the bed to the floor, which was only about a foot below.

"A little," I said, snuggling deeper into the pillow to indicate that I didn't want to get up and do anything about it.

Ivan stood up, and I looked at his strange and beautiful flesh as he headed for the shower. Decidedly too long, and too sallow. It glowed. A kind of El Greco quality about it. He was very beautiful, I decided, and cuddled deeper into the warm place our bodies had made. I dozed off.

And woke to the aroma of coffee and the sizzling sound of eggs. Ivan had showered and dressed and was standing over me, grinning, two steaming cups in his hands. He set them down and sat down beside me as I sat up sleepily, the sheet falling from around my shoulders and my hair falling into my face. I sipped the hot sweet liquid greedily. It cleared up some of the dream-fog in my head, and I stole a look at Ivan over the side of the cup. This was not the young pirate I had met in the Village the night before. Nor was it the El Greco painting I had made love to. A young man, quiet, rather, thin, dressed in clean dungarees and blue work shirt, his wet hair neatly combed. Ivan caught my eye and my thought and grinned. I grinned back. Words were not part of our thing. Then he made as if to pull me to my feet.

"Come on," he said. "The eggs will be getting cold."

I stood up and walked naked to the center of the room, where I stretched and yawned, the sunlight I had been watching all morning from the bed catching me around the ankles. I made a loose, untidy braid of my hair to keep it out of my face. Something dripped onto the instep of my foot, but I ignored it. Ivan threw me another blue denim work shirt exactly like the one he was wearing, and I put it on, rolling up the too-long sleeves and, thus attired, went in to breakfast.

We sat at a tiny table in the miniature "bachelor kitchen" and devoured frozen orange juice, fried eggs and burnt English muffins swimming in butter. Ivan had put on his glasses, which completed the transformation to a sober, rather over-serious young working man.

"Just slam the door when you go," he said, his mouth full. "It locks by itself. Stay as long as you like, play records, type, whatever." Then he added, with just a trace of hesitation, "Shall I see you tonight?"

I liked the hesitation. I liked the confidence, too, with which everything else had gone down between us, but without that hesitation he would have been just a trifle overbearing. I suppressed another grin and filled up my mouth with egg.

"I don't know," I said. "It depends. I'm still living at home."

"I'll meet you," he said. "At nine. At David's." David's was an arty coffee shop on MacDougal Street. The only one, besides the Mafia hangouts, in those days.

"OK," I said, still playing it cool. "If I'm not there, don't wait."

He gave me a long, playful look from under his eyelashes, half coaxing, half ordering me to be there, and after an eggy kiss he left for work.

Chapter 2—February Continued

I was alone in the apartment, with that particular sense of luxury that solitude always gives me. I poured myself a cup of coffee, sugared it well, and filled the cup with milk. A habit, from many times when ten cents was what I had, and a cup of coffee was going to be all of breakfast, or supper. Lots of milk and lots of sugar make it go farther, as nourishment, as energy.

I wandered over to the bookcase, selected the New Directions translation of García Lorca, and immersed myself in the elegy for Ignacio Sánchez Mejías. The electric percolator kept the coffee hot indefinitely. After a while I took another cup and wandered over to the bed. Set it down on the floor, straightened out the rumpled sheets, put a Bach cantata on the phonograph, and lay down with my book. My mind kept wandering, and after a while I put down my book and gave myself up to my thoughts.

All in all I was pretty pleased. I liked Ivan, liked his funny shyness which could pass for "being cool," liked his long skinny body, his big cock. I liked the warm, full, satisfied feeling inside me. I luxuriated in it, snuggled deeper into the soft bedding and, half-dozing, went one by one over the events of the night before.

I had been sitting in the Swing Rendezvous, a Mafia-run gay bar on MacDougal Street, with a high-school friend of mine named Susan O'Reilley. We had both run away from our respective colleges a few weeks before, and were living precariously at home, looking for jobs and apartments, and seeking refuge at night from irate parents, the police they had more than once invoked, and the entire threatening world. This bar felt "safe" to us: the fat, dumb bouncer with a Bronx accent; the skinny Mafia man with grey hair and beetling black eyebrows who sat in the back and watch over the place; the dyke waitress named Stevie Martini, so handsome and slim, with her short, bleached hair done in a d.a.; the sad little girl with big black eyes named Barbara, who worked behind the bar, and who was Stevie's girl-friend—they had come to seem almost like family in the past few weeks.

The Swing was a haven because it was off-bounds, a meeting place for outlaws. Now, in the midst of "gay liber-ation" the social stigma has gone out of homosexuality, and with it the high, bitter romanticism that made it so debonair. (I remember a hustler friend at Lenny's Hideaway one night refusing an importunate businessman with "I just don't feel that flamboyant tonight, dear.") Gayness can no longer be used to hold the world at bay, put down the soci-ety around you, signal your isolation and help you stand clear. It is no longer a component of black magic: Cocteau, Genet, or Kenneth Anger. Only last week I saw a copy of

The Well of Loneliness, secret classic of my mother's generation, selling for ten cents at a Haight Street thrift shop.

We sat in a dark wooden booth, upholstered in old red leather, our movements reflected in the speckled, blue glass mirror that lined the walls. We talked, we drank, occasionally we got up and danced with each other or with one of the "regulars," straight or gay, whom we had come to know, it seemed, almost as well as we knew each other.

The dance was the Fish, forerunner of the Twist, and much freer. You could dance it in couples, like the old folks danced the fox-trot. In that case you slipped one of your legs over one of your partner's legs, he slipped a knee into your groin, and you ground your cunt on his thigh, feeling his hard-on with your stomach or the side of your pelvis, while your hands hung casually at your sides, or were shoved into the back pockets of your jeans, the better to thrust your pelvis forward. Or you could dance it free, in twos, threes, anything up to fives: then you stomped and leaped, did back-bends, splits, pirouetted and "froze." Freezing was an art. You threw your head back, arms straight out, and as you bent slowly backward you set every muscle in your body leaping and quivering separately. Not many people could do the Freeze. All this while, your air was casual, and your face betrayed no emotion at all. The dance was the Fish, and the game was Cool.

Even in bed, I thought, the game is Cool. That side of the cantata was finished, and the record changer shuddered a little and started it over again from the beginning. Trumpets and woodwinds. A slight breeze stirred the curtain and passed over my naked body, raised goose bumps here and there as I went on thinking, sorting out the moments that had brought me here.

Susan and I had been sitting in our booth together, each huddled into a corner, talking of this and that. Susan was watching the dance floor: a young man named Claudia, who had a black streak in his blonde hair was whirling and bending to some loud rhythm-and-blues number—Dinah Washington was moaning about what it was like to sleep with her landlord. I was watching the archway that separated the bar from the back room with its tables and dancing and Cosa Nostra guardian angels. I always sat where I could watch the door. A habit. We felt safe here, sure enough, but I was prepared for anything.

Two rather beautiful young men walked in and stood in the doorway. One was somewhat taller than the other, with dark eyes, incredible eyelashes, high cheekbones, and a rather pinched look. He wore a wondrous shirt of some soft material, with a high collar open at the neck and very full sleeves with wide cuffs. His friend looked softer, younger, with light blue eyes and an expensive Italian boat-neck jersey. We had met once before a few days earlier, in David's coffee shop. I had looked up to see the taller one standing in front of my table, looking down at me. "I'm Ivan," he had said, "and this is Robin." "I'm Diane," I had replied, "and this is Susan." We had grinned at each other for a while, and they had left.

Tonight our eyes met briefly with just a flicker of recognition. Then he turned and spoke a few words to his companion. The easy way he leaned over him and the vague softness with which the younger boy looked up at him made me wonder if they were lovers. I turned to Susan to ask her what she thought, and when I looked for them again they had already gone.

I had passed my hand over the rough denim that covered Susan's knee and smiled at her. For warmth, for comfort. She squeezed my hand between her legs and smiled back. Her long, slim hand playing with the beads of moisture on her beer glass caught the dim light. Anglo-Saxon innocence, I thought. That's what she has, what she is. Big blue saucer eyes, a soft full mouth, and an uptilted nose. What made St. Augustine say that thing: "Not Anglos, but Angels."

I turned in bed, thinking about her, and slid my hand under the pillow. Blonde hair cut straight across her forehead in bangs, and falling in a soft pageboy on her rather broad, rather slim shoulders. She looked like she sang in a Methodist choir—and she had, until rather recently. Her blouse was made of some really incredible thin stuff through which you could see the pert rosebud tips of her small breasts. Her blue jeans were cut high and hugged her hips closely, and around her waist she had tied a crimson sash. I pulled the sheet up around my shoulders to keep the wind away, and wondered where Susan was at this moment. How she was doing.

What had she and I been talking about last night? I wondered. I couldn't remember, though I clearly recalled the intensity of our conversation, and the lift and joy her presence always gave me. A lilt at the heart, like sparkling wine.

I remember that a young sailor had suddenly sat down

beside me in the booth. He was all eyes for Susan. He had been drinking and was very sad. Had we ever been, he wanted to know, to Springfield, Illinois? We had never been out of New York City, except for our brief escapades at college, and Springfield could have been the moon. We told him no. He told us how he had been in love with Peggy Lee all through high school. How he had cried when he discovered she was on junk—heroin, he called it. He nearly cried again, telling us about it. Strawberry blonde hair and pink, too-chubby cheeks. Milk-fed and dumb and on his way to Korea. We were all three playing kneesies under the table when Stevie Martini came by and asked Susan to dance. She got up immediately and I was left with Mr. Middle West.

He looked after Susan sadly. "She likes girls," he announced profoundly, half to himself. Then he turned to me and repeated, "She likes girls." I said nothing about it, having nothing to say.

"Do you like girls?" he asked, trying to look deep into my eyes without falling over.

"Sometimes," I answered him.

"I like girls," he informed me drunkenly, leaning across the table. You could see he was ready to have his heart broken again, the way Peggy Lee had broken it. Then he brightened. "Let's go find three girls." He lurched to his feet and headed toward the men's room.

Frankie, an Italian racketeer of about thirty, checked in for a minute. "Honey," he said, with his thick New York accent, "is dat guy bothering you? Should I get ridda him?"

"It's OK, Frankie," I told him. "I think I can handle him OK."

Frankie went back to his post of hooker-watching. He had two little girls working for him, and one of them was currently on the dance floor. I looked after him, grateful as always for his gruff solicitude—sort of like having an extra-tough big brother.

Dreamily now, I remembered the night we had met Frankie, Susan and I. We had been walking through the Village, not exactly sure where we wanted to be, or how to get there, when he loomed in front of us, ferret face, straight black hair, and peg pants, studying us with shrewd, heroin-glazed eyes. "Don't be embarrassed, and don't be afraid," he had pronounced slowly, as if the words had some profound, cosmic meaning, as if they were some kind of oracle. "Don't be embarrassed and don't be afraid," he had repeated, blocking our path. When he told us to come with him, we had followed him without question, and he had led us to this bar which had become haven and home to us.

Susan had just sat down again when the younger of the two boys I had been watching in the doorway—Robin, I remembered—appeared suddenly at our table and spoke to me.

"My friend wants to talk to you. He asked me to ask you to come outside."

I wasn't sure whether I liked or disliked the mixture of egotism and shyness that sent this message—was it a request or an order?—into my dark, warm world. The young man standing before me was full of light. I recalled the austere beauty of his friend—the dark Tartar eyes and the narrow face—and I stood up to leave.

"I'll see you," I said to Susan. "You'll be OK?"

She took a drag on her cigarette with practiced, seventeen-year-old toughness. "I'm fine," she said. "You go ahead."

I had a few misgivings, but I squelched them. Turned back for a moment at the archway, to see Robin sitting in my seat talking to Susan, holding both her hands in his. I pushed my way through the crowd at the bar, opened the door, and stepped into the cool, fresh night air.

Wind, a sprinkling of rain. And a young man who looked like a mischievous pirate waiting for me at the bottom of a flight of wrought-iron steps.

All he said was "Hi" as he took my hand and slipped it inside his jacket pocket with his own, but his face showed relief and delight, and I was glad I hadn't quibbled over protocol. We walked through the streets and alleys in silence at first, the wet grime of the city covering our feet in their sandals. Cobblestones underfoot, slippy and slidy. Alleys with dark loading platforms, where we stopped occasionally to kiss. Foolish jokes and giddy talk, which sparkled like the rain. And in one place, a coffin standing simply, grimly, on the sidewalk outside a tenement, urging us home to warmth and love. If we had needed any urging.

We had made it up the one flight of stairs in the clean, well-painted hallway, and into the strange yellow and black apartment I was lying in now. Good, warming brandy, and Ivan slipped off my sandals and washed the city grime off my feet and his own with a hot towel. Slipped off my clothes with an awkwardness that made me trust him. Only slightly more sure of himself than I was, as I undid belt and buttons, uncovering that slim, olive-skinned body. My own whiteness gleamed in the light of that big candle, and the twenty-odd smaller candles placed here and there about the room.

The brandy set the lights to spinning around me. The brandy and his touch on my breasts. His mouth on mine as he undid my hair. I was kneeling on the straw rug, his cock in my mouth. My mouth was exploring the long smooth lines of his legs. The point of my tongue was tickling his balls, my hair fell over his feet as I nipped and fondled his ankles. He lay on the straw mat with me; we somehow got onto the bed. The world was a carousel, an amusement park full of spinning lights and loving noises. I had forgotten human speech, it stuck in my throat. I had forgotten the name of the man whose hand was in my cunt. I tugged at the hand. "Take off your ring," I said hoarsely. My voice came from Saturn and floated into the room.

He was on me now, bucking and straining like an animal. A faun. But it was too much. My small tight cunt couldn't take in his huge cock. His urgency, demanding, threw me off. I struggled against it. He buried his face in my hair. "Lie still," he said in my ear. "Lie still and listen to the rain."

I went limp, I floated in a soft, grey mist. The room dissolved, had the candles gone out? I saw nothing. His long beautiful hands under my buttocks drew me closer to him. I embraced him with my thighs, locked my ankles around his back. I knew I was drowning, I could taste the sea. I could hear my own voice crying out as he pierced the membrane that protected my virginity, but I was unaware that I had spoken. The grey mist exploded in light and color around me. I could hear myself moaning, I could hear Ivan gasp. Over and over again he whispered my name, and then there was nothing left but pleasure I had never imagined surging through me in wave after wave.

Afterward there was blood on his cock, and when I could move again I licked it off, swallowing my childhood, entering the world of the living.

Chapter 3—February Concluded

The sudden silence woke me up. Someone had turned off the phonograph and the Bach cantata that had been resounding through my reveries had come to an abrupt end. Someone had turned off the phonograph. I half sat up, leaning on one elbow, and looked to see who was in the room.

The day had grown overcast, and as the apartment got no afternoon light, it was quite dim. Somebody was rattling around in the kitchen.

"Hello," I said, feeling it out.

"Hello," said Robin, emerging into the larger room. The light was on in the kitchen, silhouetting him against the doorway. He looked larger than I remembered, but that might be because the bed was on the floor and I was looking up at him.

"Oh, it's you," I said. "How's Susan? Is she here?"

"No," he said, "I dropped her off at home a little while ago. She said she'd call you. Thought you'd be home by now."

"No," I said. "I went back to sleep."

A natural teenage urge to get on the phone and chatter it all away came over me and I was thinking about getting up and doing just that when Robin sat down beside me on the mattress.

"You're beautiful," he said. "Your hair." He lay down beside me, fully clothed, and spread it over his face. I lay undecided, half awakened now, and wanting to get up and start a day, and yet . . . He did seem very beautiful and young, looking at me across the pillow with vague baby-blue eyes.

"Your hair is beautiful," he said, bunching it in his hand and pulling it away from my face, "and yet when it goes away, I look across the pillow and see a beautiful young boy."

A trip. My old longing to be a pirate, tall and slim and hard, and not a girl at all. He saw a beautiful young boy, and I lay still to listen.

But he had nothing else to say. Instead he moved somehow across the pillow and kissed me. Not at all like Ivan's kiss—vaguer and somehow sadder.

"Hey," I said gently, "hey." I touched the side of his face with my hand. I slid my hand under his neck and drew him closer to me. I kissed him again, longer and more thoroughly, showing him how, a hundred hows he had forgotten, or never known.

His hand slipped under the sheet and examined my breast shyly. Then drew away and slid over my ribs, down my back. Played for a long time with my buttocks, really liked them. Their smoothness. Traced curves from hip to navel, then back again, searching gently the dark crease

24

between the two mounds of my ass. He drew his hand away, sticky with half-dried come that had flowed there from my morning of lovemaking. He threw the sheet back and made marks on my hips with the wetness. Ivan's wetness, I could feel him thinking. I said nothing, but I had a thousand questions in my head.

Robin bent his head to my bared body, and took one of my breasts into his mouth. Deliberately. Trying it out. I curled my fingers in his hair, pressing him to me, half in pleasure, half in a vague attempt to comfort him for I knew not what.

As I held him so, I thought of the many strange, half-finished scenes I had found myself in during the past two years, since I had first allowed myself to be picked up at the age of fifteen on the way home from a modern dance class. Many were the experiments I had engaged in and abruptly stopped, many the love scenes I had witnessed or aided, but I had always been put off by the blasé, professional quality of my partners, and had not been willing to "go all the way" till last night, when Ivan's beauty and awkwardness had completely won me over. All odds and ends of sexual skill which my seventeen-year-old self had accumulated, and which last night had been completely blasted out of my grasp by the intensity of our coming together, now returned, demanding to be tried and tested. This boy, more frightened and hungry than I had ever been, called them out of me.

It was strange to feel his clothing against me, buttons pressed into my belly and groin. I longed to undress him, to see his white, almost hairless torso, but I didn't know what he wanted, how much or how little, and somehow hesitated for fear I might frighten him off. This was, I reflected, a little sleepily, his shot. My fingers stroked the nape of his neck and under his collar. He withdrew his lips from my nipple and, cupping both my breasts in his hands, buried his head between them, slowly working his way down the length of my torso.

I could feel the zipper of his pants scratch my thigh, his hard cock under it. He began to lick my stomach, the hair of my pussy, stiff with my come and Ivan's, deliberately, hungrily, tasting and devouring, pausing to sniff and smell at my thighs. He parted my buttocks slightly and licked at the come that was caught in the hair there, drawing all my hairs through his lips till they became soft again and curling. Then he began to lick the bud of my clitoris, first taking from it, too, the dried juices of my earlier lovemaking, and then finally paying attention to it for its own sake, caught up at last in the act he was engaged in.

His brusque tentativeness and my own sleepiness cut through defenses I didn't know I still had, and, as he tongued my pink bud, I thrashed and moaned above him, throwing my hands above my head and clutching the top edge of the mattress while my body arched and shivered.

At last he moved slightly and brought his mouth against the lips of my cunt, gently parting them with his tongue, and sucking long and deep of the juices gathered inside me. Ivan's come, I again sensed him thinking. I could feel his mounting excitement in his hands as, all unconscious, they raked my sides, leaving the marks of his nails in my flanks. His tongue felt warm and curiously comfortable against the slightly sore skin of my cunt as he stroked first one wall and then the other. My excitement, which had abated slightly when his tongue left my clitoris, began to mount again and, as his straining tongue passed deeper into my opening, I began to jerk and leap, grasping his head tightly between my thighs while I let flow into his mouth the juices of my reawakened pleasure.

I lay still for some time, waiting for the soft shivering in my skin to stop, feeling the waves of chill that left my skin in goosebumps and my nipples hard and high, the drawing, subtle sweetness in my groin, while my fingers played idly in Robin's soft brown hair. The quality of this experience was completely different from anything that I had felt with Ivan—this time I had remained fully conscious and release had been gentle and prolonged. I wondered abstractly whether that would qualify as an orgasm, having been trained by Wilhelm Reich to think in terms of the graphs in his illegal books, with their clear and well-drawn peaks. I was not yet acquainted with the infinite gradations and subtleties of pleasure. I gave it up, and withdrew into the misty sleepiness and vague music in my head.

At last Robin raised his head and looked at me, full of the light I had longed to turn on in him. "You are a veil," he said, "through which we make love to each other."

I did not ask how or who, I had already read his love for Ivan, and as I drew him up toward me with small urgent movements of my hand, I wondered merely if it was unfulfilled. If they were making it or not. So many questions.

I didn't ask—the game was Cool, remember—but made as if to coax him gently to me, till his eyes were level with

27

mine. We lay for a long time wordless, looking across the pillow at each other, my arm under his neck, my hand fondling his shoulder through the stuff of his shirt. After a while, by some slight sign, some imperceptible change in his breathing, I realized that his own desire was mounting. My free hand found his fly and, looking him lovingly in the eyes, I released his hard cock—smaller than Ivan's but still the strong developed member of a man. It gave the lie to the angelic, childlike quality of his face and figure. I slid my hand in through the opening in his shorts and felt of his full balls, stroking and smoothing the wrinkled skin gently, and then drawing my fingers over the full length of his prick with the lightest of all possible touches, gentling him as I would a wild creature I wished to tame. Over and over I drew my hand down the length of his cock, as it became longer and began to buck in my grasp.

Robin moaned. His eyes were shut, and his head, thrown back, showed his long, beautiful neck and the slight protuberance of his Adam's apple. I was spent, totally satisfied, and therefore fully in control of the situation. I moved my head deliberately across the pillow and sank my teeth into that white neck just above the collarbone, sucking and tonguing the place I had chosen. OK, I thought, I am vampire and you are my chosen victim, and I will drink your blood till you lie pale and still. Pleasure stirred in me again as I toyed with this fantasy, and my hand continued to fondle his balls. His moan turned into a gasp of anguish and pleasure, and just as suddenly as I had begun I withdrew my mouth from his neck and my hand from his cock. I had decided to undress him.

A sound half hiss, half whimper escaped from between his teeth. "Please, don't stop now," he pleaded, and he drew my hand back to his organs. But I pulled away and continued to work on his shirt till I opened it, exposing his white, almost hairless chest—pale, paler than I was, but without the unholy magic of Ivan's sallow flesh. I set my teeth into the flesh of his right breast, just above the nipple, and left a small half-circle of purple tooth marks there, while my fingers undid his belt and tugged at his trousers.

He raised his hips passively, and I drew his pants down over them and left them tangled about his thighs as I went back to stroking and pulling his cock, finally closing my fingers around it and moving my hand faster and faster while his body bucked and trembled. My other arm had by now slipped down around his waist and, as I felt him near a climax, I slipped the middle finger of that hand into his tight, dry asshole. With an exquisite, bewildered child-cry of mingled agony and pleasure, he came. I watched spurt after spurt of the hot, silver jism fall across my stomach and form a web on my pubic hair.

It was some time before his gasping and shuddering had stopped, and we both floated for a while in a haze of satisfaction and peace that was very like napping in the afternoon light.

I was the first to recover. I raised myself on one elbow and looked at him for a long time, toying with the idea of getting up, of more coffee, wondering what the outside world felt like, was it cold or not? The young man lay there with his eyes peacefully shut, his rumpled clothes still clinging to, and concealing, most of him. Suddenly, the aggressiveness I had felt when I thrust my finger into his asshole and felt his hot come on my groin rose in me again. I wanted to set his body trembling under my hands, to play it like an instrument. I was keenly aware of the absurdity of its half-clothed state, which roused me still more.

I slid down in the bed and began to undo his shoes, slipping them off so that they fell softly to the floor. I slipped my fingers under his socks and played with the backs of his ankles—smooth and wondrously thin. I stripped off black nylon socks and took one extraordinarily white foot in my hands, feeling the smooth skin of instep, massaging it lightly with strong fingers before I bent and drew my tongue along the ridge of the arch. Robin was not fully awake, and when I reached up to pull off his trousers he did not protest, but helped me by raising himself slightly on the bed. The hair on his legs was fine and calves supple and elongated like a dancer's. I traced their lines with my fingers, following along the hollows they made, raising the soft hair like fur and then smoothing it down again. I felt thoughtful, impersonal, as if I were making love in the abstract.

The past day and night were blurred into one long flesh experience. I felt it had gone on eternally. I was weary, removed, light-headed, but still infinitely curious.

I dropped the trousers on the floor beside the shoes and socks, and turned my attention to removing his shirt. He raised himself slightly and slipped out of it himself, flipping over in bed as he did so, with a gesture half shy, half coy, so that he lay face down, his head buried in the pillow. I knelt on the mattress, sitting back on my heels, and began to play the tips of my fingers over the smooth skin of his back and ass, watching the gooseflesh rise beneath my touch while he lay immobile.

I traced every inch of back and side and flank with a touch as light as butterfly wings, slowly, deliberately. I gradually let my touch get rougher, till I was scraping the pale surface of his body with my fingernails, rousing and irritating every inch of his skin. Robin began to stir with pleasure, raising himself under my hands, purring like a cat. I played a long time with the nape of his neck, alternately smoothing and scratching it. At last I brought my mouth into play, leaving a series of marks down the back of his neck and his spine, then tonguing and licking all of his back. A trail of wetness, like the path of a snail, grew and curved over his skin, already marked with the long red parallel paths of my fingernails.

I passed my lips lightly over his hairless hips, placing the side of one of my hands in the dark crease between his buttocks, as my mouth moved on down over the backs of his thighs and lingered for a long time at the skin at the back of his knees, while a weird sorry tenderness overtook me. He raised his ass against the side of my hand, so that it penetrated more deeply into that dark, hairy crease, and as I realized where the focus of his pleasure lay, I turned my attention more fully to it, parting the two mounds of his buttocks till I found his small, round asshole.

All right, I thought, I am certainly not Ivan, but I will give you what pleasure I can. Overcoming a momentary revulsion, I set my mouth over it, licking and reaming the opening, while Robin trembled from head to foot, clutching at the mattress. I raised my head, threw one knee over him so that I straddled his body and, sitting back on his upper thighs which I grasped tightly between my knees, I thrust first one and then two fingers deep into the dark hole, now slick with my saliva. Robin moaned, and, as the second finger entered him, cried out with pain, thrashing from side to side, and bucking his ass up and down wildly. I bent my head down to the small of his back and bit him till I drew blood, tasting the salty liquid again and again, while my right hand plunged up and down in his anus and my left hand raked welts across his shoulders. At last I withdrew, kneeling upright as I straddled him, and drinking in the desperate moans and convulsive trembling that I had set going, aware at last of the turmoil of emotions within myself: desire, aroused by the power I was wielding, and anguish and frustration that I could not complete the act I was approximating, that I was not the man—pirate or jewel thief—I had so often in the daydreams of adolescence pretended to myself to be. Suddenly I was angry at Robin for desiring Ivan, for taking no pleasure in my flesh for its own sake.

I set my hands on his shoulders and turned him over. He resisted momentarily, but I dug my nails into his shoulders and he, limp with uncompleted pleasure and agony, did as I wished. His member was huge and sprang up erect as soon as it was released from its imprisonment. Still kneeling over him, I thrust my fingers deep into my wet cunt, separating the lips and lowering my hole over the dark swollen head of his prick. Smaller than Ivan's, it fitted comfortably into my slightly sore, still tight cunt. I remained thus motionless for a moment, drinking in the pleasure of this comfortable fullness, and then I reached down to play with his balls and find once more his raked and painful asshole. I began to buck slowly up and down, riding him as he turned his head from side to side in pain and pleasure, seeking to bury his face once more in the pillow. My finger, now wet with my own juice, was once again deep in his anus, describing small circles and I could sense the sharp heightening of his pleasure as my fingernail for a moment caught accidentally against the sensitive skin.

At last my weariness and satiation were overcome and I was fully roused by the helpless anguish and ecstasy of the boy beneath me. My movements became uncontrollable, shaking my whole torso, and unearthly animal sounds burst from my lips as I passed my free hand over his twisted face. For a brief moment I felt that I was drinking his entire being into my cunt as he pumped his life juice into me and I fell forward, face downward, against his chest.

Chapter 4—April

The dappled sunlight filtering through the leaves outside fell through the open doorway and across my bare instep. I curled my toes inside the old black ballet slipper and stirred (I thought) imperceptibly.

"Don't move," said Tomi. She frowned, poking around in a small wooden box beside her, and came up with a Conté crayon.

"OK," I said, "just a couple minutes more. I'm getting stiff."

We were in a huge and beautiful barn which had been converted into a studio, on the edge of some woods just outside of Darien, Connecticut. If I raised my head just slightly I could see the bare beams of the ceiling with its skylight of frosted glass set to catch the north light. The walls had been "finished" in plaster-board nailed over the old wood and painted a glaring white. At my back was a huge picture window cut in the old barn wall with a burlap drape now drawn so as to diffuse the sunlight and make a background for the sketch in progress. The floor was old-

fashioned wide-planked pine, newly laid and rather beautiful. I rubbed a board with my toe appreciatively, inclining
my head just slightly to look at the grain.

"OK, DiPrima, OK, just a minute," said Tomi with a
laugh that was half self-amusement, half annoyance.

I collected myself, held still, and gave myself up to
studying the girl before me.

She was small, even smaller than I was, with short, dark
hair, and, even at eighteen, an intense, intensely wasted
face. Her hands as she drew were very beautiful: small,
strong, nervous as they traced line after quick line on the
rough paper. Her short hair was curly; one lock fell over her
face as she drew, and as I watched, her wide, mobile mouth
formed those expressions of self-criticism and self-absorp-
tion that I had come to know so well.

An aura hung about her which was an aura of everything we had done and experienced together: the long,
sleepy winter afternoons at college when both of us had lain
together in my small dormitory room, listening to the
Brahms *Requiem* while the acrid smell of burning leaves
drifted in through the window, and we alternately dallied
and dozed, till one of us, roused to desire, fell upon the
other with hungry mouth and guided a willing hand home
to her cunt.

Or the afternoons, not less frequent, when five or six
girls had gathered in one room. One had been chosen and
ritually stripped, and the rest, posted at different parts of
her anatomy, sought to arouse her while she lay naked on
the bed. Those long school days spent in studying, though
what we studied was not the prescribed curriculum: Tomi

playing, for instance, with Kate's feet and ankles, while I nibbled at her small breasts, and Lee, whom we both loved, licked at her belly and finally her cunt—those days formed now a scent and taste about us, leaving the air in a room heavy and charged when we both entered it.

I could feel the electricity flow through my limbs and into my loins as I thought of these things, could feel the aching hunger and slight moistness in my cunt. Tomi sensed what I was feeling, or else my expression changed, for she put down the Conté crayons, set aside her drawing board, and came to me. Our mouths met, I ran my fingers through her short, dark hair, and made as if to lie with her on the wide-planked floor of the studio. But she resisted, shaking her head.

"Martha will see us." Martha was her mother.

"Fuck Martha," I said, not for the first time. "Let's shut the barn door."

"Then she'll know, for sure."

Tomi started to slip away, but I still had her by the waist and drew her to me where I sat, slipping my hand under her white man-tailored blouse and feeling of the charged, mobile flesh of her small back. My face was buried now in her neck and, as I held onto her waist with one hand, I fumbled to open her grey flannel slacks with the other.

"Di Prima, goddammit, don't!"

There was real fright in her voice and I let her go, half trembling with the smell of her—Chanel's *Russian Leather*, her habitual cologne—which was to haunt me for the rest of my life.

Tomi stood half a foot away from me, tucking her

blouse back into her slacks, straightening her ascot tremulously, all without raising her big green eyes to mine. At last she turned her back on me, whipped out a comb, and combed her boyish locks back into place. Then, very slowly and meticulously, she arranged the Conté crayons in their box, closed it, picked up a can of fixative, sprayed her drawing and stood it on an easel to dry, while I stood watching her, half angry and half amused.

When at last she turned toward me the flush in her cheeks had subsided, leaving her very pale and very grave. She held out her hand with a smile that begged me not to be angry: "Come on, di Prima, we'll go for a walk in the woods."

The woods began just a few yards beyond the barn, and once in them and out of the sun it was damp, with the damp chilliness of early spring. The ground was soft, the green moss on the tree trunks shone like jewels. I picked my way carefully in my old ballet shoes, trying to avoid really sharp rocks and soggy places. I was wearing a pair of blue jeans pulled over a black leotard and bound about with a royal blue sash. My hair was loose and kept getting caught in the branches and my bare feet in their slippers were chilly.

We forded a stream. That is, Tomi, forded it easily enough in her loafers. I, being a city girl, didn't even try: I slipped off my soggy slippers and stepped right into the icy, fast-running water. The stream was quite shallow and not very wide, but when I stepped out my feet and ankles were white as parchment, two of my toes were numb, and the bottoms of my jeans were dripping. The far bank of the stream sloped slightly and we clambered up, slipping and sliding, laughing and pelting each other with leaves and pieces of bark.

At last the ground grew drier, it leveled off, and we came to a clearing full of sunshine where a few huge boulders lay basking and sunning themselves. I climbed a rock and lay down on my back in the sun, one arm thrown over my eyes to shield them and my wet muddy shoes set beside me to dry. I could feel the warmth from the stone soak into my body, could hear the headlong rush of the stream full of melted snow, and the soft, hesitant rustles and occasional birdcalls of the woodland creatures in my self-created darkness.

Tomi came and lay at right angles to me, and put her head on my stomach. Every muscle in my body thrilled and tensed, but I didn't move. I could feel my flesh grow alternately warm and cold where her breath, filtering through my nylon leotard, touched my skin.

We lay together for a long time without speaking and then—her lips lightly brushing my stomach as she did so—she turned her head so that she was facing my feet. She reached one slim, small-muscled arm down along my leg, brushing my ankle with the tips of her fingers.

"You're still wet from the stream," she murmured. She pushed my damp dungarees further up my legs and, sliding down, began to suck the droplets of water that clung to my ankles. At last I stirred, took the arm from across my eyes and, raising my head slightly, looked down at the small dark creature who could arouse such sorrow and hunger in me.

"Still wet, and muddy," I answered her.

She rose to her knees and sat back on her heels, looking

at me with an agony of hunger, behind which lurked a certain lewd playfulness.

"I'll fix that in a minute," she muttered and, raising her hands to her blouse, began to unbutton it as swiftly and matter-of-factly as possible.

She slipped it off, folded it, and placed it beside her on the rock, while I took in the familiar, creamy texture of her skin: its delicate, off-white ivory color against which the pristine whiteness of her brassiere stood out starkly. A swift movement of her hands behind her back and she had slipped it off, and I studied her burnt-sienna nipples and the heaviness of her young breasts, which sagged ever so slightly in spite of her scant eighteen years.

She was still on her knees beside me, but now, with a single motion, she stood up and began to undo her slacks. She slipped them off, together with her underpants, as easily and unself-consciously as if she was undressing alone in her own bedroom. She separated the slacks and the panties, folded the slacks and placed them neatly, her cotton panties on top. She stepped out of her loafers and, her back to me, bent to remove her heavy wool socks, so that for a brief moment I was aware of nothing but the dark crease of her ass and the red slit beyond, where a small bead of creamy moisture had already gathered.

Then she straightened and, making fists of her hands, stretched them straight above her head, throwing her face back toward the sun and standing on tiptoe as she stretched out her whole torso in an almost ritual movement. The concave place in the small of her back was matched by the concave line under her rib cage as her stomach flattened and flexed in narcissistic pleasure under the warm sun.

I studied her small figure—the wide hips and heavy breasts so lush in spite of her slimness, the warm tone of her flesh—seeking to find the combination of elements, of color and line, that bound me to her: that had done so for the two years I had known her.

She looked down at me where I lay on the rock in a welter of red hair, no longer sulking but still distant and wary.

"Still wet and muddy," she drawled mockingly, and then, kneeling again at my feet, began gently, half-teasingly, to dry my ankles with her white cotton panties. She dried them slowly, alternating left and right, first my ankles, then my insteps, then the arch of each foot; then she began to wipe the mud from the soles of my feet and to clean and dry my toes one by one, wiping the mud from between them with her underwear, finally bending and taking them into her mouth.

I lay under her ministrations, feeling her touch on the soft skin of my feet, not moving while wave after wave of desire swept over me. At last I could contain myself no longer, and I sat up and drew her to me, drinking deeply of her scents: cologne and hair, sweat and lust, all mingling in a fragrance that was Tomi, as I kissed her soft, acquiescent mouth again and again.

Her small hands slipped behind my back and under my hair and unzipped my leotard and unhooked my bra so that she could, with one motion, slip them both down over my shoulders. Still holding my mouth with her own, she drew me to my feet, undid my jeans, and with my eager help slipped all my clothes off in one tangled heap. I stepped out of them without interrupting our kiss.

We stood there together on our rock in the sun, and I shivered as the cool damp breeze of early spring came out of the woods and found us. My head bent to hers, our bodies scarcely touching, and I raised one hand and gently began to stroke one of her breasts, while the other hand found its way between her thighs. She contrived to separate them slightly, and I lightly rubbed her clitoris, feeling it stand out and harden slightly under my touch, before I slid my fingers into that warm, moist cunt I knew so well.

She sank her weight slightly upon my hand so as to draw me even further into her, and I played with the walls of her opening, exploring here and there, steadily, eagerly, while my other hand slipped from her breast and went around her shoulders, half supporting, half embracing her. Both her arms were around me; her hands hooked onto my shoulders helped to hold her up. Then my plunging, trembling hand touched the neck of her womb, and she bit down on my lower lip with a moan, her pelvis jerking wildly.

With one sharp cry she released a flood of come over my hand and collapsed against me. I nearly staggered under her weight, but managed to keep my balance as she leaned against me, her flushed face buried against my chest, her breasts and stomach totally crushed against me. As she so often did when we reached a climax, she was crying softly to herself.

I withdrew my hand softly, and she, her crying abating somewhat, slipped to her knees in front of me and raised her mouth to my cunt.

I stood over her, squatting slightly to allow her easier

access to my throbbing, aching cunt. Her tongue flickered ceaselessly, maddeningly over my clitoris, her arms were around my thighs, her hands on my buttocks squeezed them convulsively. My excitement had almost passed the point of being pleasurable, the sun was whirling in the sky, I felt that I could no longer stand. I bent almost double, clutching her short black hair in both hands, as my head hung down and I whispered her name.

At last her tongue entered my cunt, moving in and out with quick, sure strokes. I could feel her teeth press against my pelvic bone as she strove to enter more deeply. The walls of my vagina were quivering, vibrating like an exquisitely tuned instrument to her every stroke and nuance. At last everything went totally black, a familiar fire licked from my stomach down into my groin and with long, racking shudders I came into her mouth.

I don't know how I got down, but I found myself lying beside her. Her head was still level with my crotch and there was a small purple bruise beginning to show on my hip, where my bone had struck a rock. It had grown chilly, and even as I stroked her head and shoulders I wondered how I could get to my clothes without disturbing the girl whose head lay on my thigh.

She stirred first, groping though the pockets of her slacks for a cigarette, lighting it with nervous, nicotine-stained fingers. The sun was getting low, and now that the spell was broken warmth became the only imperative. I sat up and fumbled my way back into my clothes, cursing and mumbling as I slipped my feet into my cold, wet shoes. Tomi spoke once, hopefully, to suggest the swimming hole, but I cut her off by saying it was too cold, and it was.

We tromped back, rumpled and peaceful, and just as we got to the barn dusk was falling and the first stars were out.

We closed up the studio in silence, pausing only for a brief kiss. Tomi picked up the sketch she had done that afternoon—to show Martha—and we walked across the field to the small farmhouse whose windows were casting chunks of bright light across the evening. The curtains were not drawn, and even before we entered the house we could see that Serge, Tomi's father, was busy preparing drinks, that Martha was knitting something black in front of the fire, that her brother William was back at work on his hi-fi kit.

We entered with muttered excuses, and ducked quickly into Tomi's room to wash and dress—make ourselves more or less presentable for the evening—pausing often to touch and fondle, to laugh and whisper together.

Chapter 5—April Continued

I had met Tomi when I had first gone to college, about a year and a half before. After the joyous and rather surreal freedom of high school in Manhattan, college had, on the whole, been a crashing disappointment: a place of male and female stereotypes in cashmere sweaters, and of raucous, ugly beer parties. A place of unhappy faculty members casting sidelong glances at lascivious virgins from Little Rock. A place of endless bridge games, fudge parties, ennui which spread like the plague over a rather beautiful campus and into every nook and cranny of the ivy-covered buildings. A good place for a murder, certainly, which saw instead an average of three suicides a semester.

There had been, however, saving grace in the person of a few interesting personalities—all women, as it happened—landmarks which kept one from stepping off the edge into the abyss of boredom and despair that was always spread out before one in those days, like one of Bosch's panoramic visions.

There was Mara, long and German, with her green

eyes, her beautiful figure, her fuzzy brown hair, her under-stated civilization. Her uncle Max was a famous essayist and left wing culture hero.

There was Matilda, whose cloud of red-gold hair spread a radiance around her almost-six-foot frame, whose lush, well-stacked figure gave the lie to her innocence.

There was Kate, whose shrill, talkative voice and angular form were well compensated by the insatiable quality of her desire and her willingness to give pleasure. Kate came from the wilds of the wild west, somewhere outside of Seattle, another planet altogether, of whose existence we had heard vague rumors, but of whose language and culture, customs and manners, we had no idea at all.

There was Lee, a very beautiful, partially deaf girl with an angry Dutch father and a sad, gentle Indonesian mother, who had lived in a pre-Revolutionary inn in eastern Massachusetts until she had come away to school. Lee, who had once been raped in a field by one of her father's hired hands and frequently bullwhipped in the barn by her father, could not bear to be touched at all.

And then there was Tomi. Tomi, who galvanized the whole scene and made it come alive, by falling in love with each of us, one after the other.

To each of the others in our close, intense scene I could relate to some extent—there was some area in which their lives and mine overlapped, in which their values met my own—but with Tomi I had no point of reference at all, and so of course it was with her that I fell in love. I suspect that we all did, and for the same reason.

The inside of Tomi's head was full of harpsichords and

ink washes, tweeds and lust. Her letters were amazing, eclectic compositions which owed much to Dylan Thomas and J. D. Salinger for their style, and to Jean Cocteau and Jean Paul Sartre for their content. I had just come from a world of Puccini and Tchaikovski to Bach; she played me Schuetz and Palestrina and found Bach "too ornate." Her clothes were a wistful approximation of Bergdorf Goodman and Abercrombie & Fitch. When she spoke of an apartment in New York it was in the West Village, was stark white, with skylights and Swedish glass, black sling chairs which she called "African camp chairs."

Her parents who had no more money than my own, lived beyond their means in expensive Darien, and shopped in a Gristede's where everything cost three times as much as it did in the local supermarket in Brooklyn, but where Tallulah Bankhead could be seen buying brandied peaches. Tomi's mother Martha was a handsome little woman in her mid-forties, Anglo-Saxon and proper, grim and laconic, a woman who did what was expected of her, and took no pleasure in it. It was a well-known—and frequently discussed—fact within the family circle that she was frigid. Her father was a florid Latin type, half French and half Italian, who drank emotionally, spent too much money, and was openly and despairingly in love with his wife. Their dogs were mangy, but thoroughbred; their heroes F. Scott Fitzgerald and Harry Crosby. Their house was much too small, their barn too big; they read *The New Yorker* and the Sunday *Times*, lived on peanut butter sandwiches and scrambled eggs, and drank endless martinis in front of the fireplace in their dark, crowded living room.

All this was an astonishment to me. I came from Brooklyn, from a block that just avoided being a slum, where I had played stickball in the street and dodged the Irish altar boys. My parents were first-generation Americans, my grandparents Italian, and our backyard was full of grapevines and tomato plants. I had seventeen aunts and as many uncles, and twenty-two first cousins, whom I had been taught to regard as additional brothers and sisters. My grandparents could not read or write; my parents, with grim determination, had put themselves through college and become "professional people." They were never in debt and bought nothing "on time." They were noisy and unpretentious: the cupboard was always full and the liquor cabinet (if there was one) was usually empty except for homemade wine. To like to drink hard liquor was considered a misfortune.

Our feasts and festivals had been hearty peasant affairs, at which, ever since I was twelve, I had found myself dodging the amorous advances of a portly uncle, who was ostensibly teaching me the tango; at which I had had to stand for inspection while my grandmother and my mother's older sisters felt of my budding breasts, drawing them out with their fingers, or spanned my bottom with their hands, while commenting in Italian on my good and bad points as a future breeding animal. All this was done in a spirit of utter kindness and delight. No one of my thirty-four aunts or uncles had ever been heard to complain of their sex life or marriage—it would have been an inconceivable breach of etiquette—except for unfortunate Aunt Zelda, whose husband had simply left her, and who therefore could no longer pretend to be happy whether she was or not.

And so it was with total amazement that, on my first visit to Tomi in her home, I heard a drunk Serge list the accumulated woes of his home and marriage. This first astonishment was followed by a second even greater one when, on opening my eyes the next morning on an Army cot in the living room, I found myself accepting from Serge a rather large martini, complete with olive. Everyone was flitting about in their nightclothes, everyone was drinking. I drank one martini, and then two. I was more than slightly tipsy and *very* hungry when Serge handed me a third.

"Oh, dear," I exclaimed, more or less involuntarily, "such a chore, swallowing them, one after the other!" This ingenuous remark endeared me to the entire company. I was "in."

However, no one mentioned breakfast. After a while people dispersed to sketch, or fish, or sew; Serge settled down to some serious drinking; no one ate at all. And so the day went by.

As many days had since. I had by now become used to the ways of the household, and thoroughly enjoyed my visits, as one might enjoy visiting the household of a family of fantastically well-bred Venusians. With the added complication that I was, had been, and (I was convinced) evermore would be, in love with one of the aforementioned girl-Venutians.

So much in love that, sitting with her and O'Reilley in Arthur's Tavern in the West Village a few months before, I had willingly agreed to leave school and join them in getting an apartment, although I knew that they were currently in love with each other. So much in love that, at Tomi's request, I had broken off with Ivan without a word to him. Well, here I was, I had found an apartment, I would tell Tomi about it tomorrow, and a new scene, our scene, would start: bamboo and burlap, white walls, black furniture. Drawing tables for Tomi's commercial art, which was, theoretically at least, going to support us. Russel Wright dishes. Pepperidge Farm bread and lamb chops.

So here indeed I definitely was, I reflected with as much gravity as I could muster after four drinks. I sat down to the dinner table with the entire Klebert crew, hearing the phonograph slow down and speed up, and watching the floor tilt in its accustomed fashion.

Martha passed the burnt pot roast, one of her culinary feats, and we each took one thin slice. William, Tomi's fourteen-year-old brother ("Sweet William" they usually called him) passed the instant mashed potatoes. Serge poured everyone some bourbon on the rocks, and "Aunt Helen," Serge's sister, stuck a rhinestone hatpin into her chignon.

It was all I could do to keep from bursting into shouts of delight. I stepped on Tomi's foot under the table and got an "I love you" poke in the shins in response, while she choked on her salad.

"What are we doing tomorrow?" asked Sweet William, through a thick blob of potato.

"I thought we might take the boat out," said Serge, "and have a picnic on the island."

Martha groaned and rolled her eyes to the ceiling, but said nothing.

Aunt Helen fairly chortled with joy: "Wonderful! I

heard the weather report, and there are storm warning for Long Island Sound. It should be a *marvelous* trip!" Her bridgework gleamed in the indirect lighting and her chignon bobbed with excitement.

After supper Helen, who was some kind of a witch, offered to read the Tarot for me. Martha had gone back to her knitting and Serge, having finished the bourbon, had switched to cognac. I cut the cards and Tomi and William and I watched while she laid them out with some ceremony.

"Martha," said Tomi, on whom the occult weighed heavily, and who was, therefore, desirous of breaking the spell, "can we afford to get me another basic black at Bonwit's?"

There it was again, *The New Yorker*, complete with alliteration. A quick glance at Tomi told me she was perfectly serious.

"We can afford," Martha grated with more asperity than usual, her eyes on the depleted cognac bottle, "to get you a basic black loincloth. That's all."

Charles Addams, I thought, that's what it all reminds me of. I turned back to Helen. She was gazing at the cards in horror. Even her eyeglasses quivered.

"Don't ask me to read this, darling!" she cried, laying a pitying hand on my arm, and fixing awestruck eyes on me. "I cannot tell you what I see."

"OK," I said, suspecting a shuck.

Serge was lying on the rug at Martha's feet next to the dog.

"Martha, Martha, lovely Martha. Lovely Martha,

Martha, Martha," he intoned again and again. Martha merely pursed her lips and went on knitting.

He got up unsteadily and bent over her, reeking no doubt of alcohol, and made as if to kiss her. She eluded him with practiced skill and got up to poke the fire. Suddenly he straightened, a gleam came into his eyes, and he rushed out of the house, picking up the shotgun that stood by the door on his way.

Dead silence settled on the house. Martha sat down and went on with her knitting. Helen continued to pick up the Tarot cards and put them back in the deck. Tomi sat still and very white, watching her.

A sharp retort and then another. The gun had been fired. The dog stood up and made for the door, growling low in his throat. Martha put down her knitting.

Tomi rushed to her. "Don't go out there!" she cried.

Martha looked horrified. The idea of going out there had never occurred to her.

Helen went instead, and a moment later Serge lurched back into the room, putting his hand through a glass doorpane as he did so. His only injury. He had "missed" twice with the gun—probably fired it into the air.

And then at last, Martha stirred. She stood up. She moved with fast, funereal step into the kitchen. She emerged with a sponge and began to follow Serge as he wandered and ranted, mopping up the blood that dripped from his cut hand. She did not look once at Serge, or at any of the rest of us, but simply at her floor, and she followed him, cleaning, cleaning, cleaning, from room to room.

"Something should be done about that cut," said

Helen, turning to me as presumably the only other sane one in the house. (Sweet William had by then disappeared. He was probably hiding under his bed—his favorite refuge in times of stress. And Tomi still sat at the card table, immobile and white as a sheet.)

"It is bleeding rather heavily," I replied as tritely as possible. I was fighting a desire to giggle.

"Do you think you could—?"

I shook my head gravely, trying to seem heavy with responsibility.

"He'll never hold still for it," I answered. "Better wait till he quiets down."

Serge was spouting some rhetoric about how badly he was wounded, but how he would give his life for "lovely Martha." He flung his arms about as he shouted, spattering blood on the walls.

At last he wandered into the kitchen, tripped over the ironing board, and fell on the floor beside the dishwasher. I seized the opportunity and with one flying leap landed on his chest, where I sat firmly.

"Yes, Serge," I said, as I seized the injured hand and held it aloft for Helen to bandage, "you certainly are very brave. No one could ask for more. But you must rest. Lovely Martha is crying to see how you've worn yourself out."

Martha made a grimace and studied her dirty sponge.

"You must rest, Serge, " I continued, while Helen cut adhesive tape efficiently, "because tomorrow . . ." but he was by then snoring on the floor.

Martha contemplated him coldly for a moment, then stepped over him and rinsed out her sponge at the kitchen sink.

I got off him gingerly, a little disappointed that my performance had been so abruptly curtailed. I felt tired.

Helen poured four cognacs thoughtfully. "Well," she said, "well, well, well. I'm certainly glad he didn't hurt himself."

Tomi wasn't in the living room. I took my cognac in one hand and hers in the other and went off in search of her.

She wasn't in her room either, but as I started back down the hall I heard low but unmistakably amorous sounds coming from William's room. I put my ear to the door.

"Slow now, ohhh, slow, Sweet William, yes, like that . . . Oh, god."

Tomi had no doubt gone in search of her upset brother and was even now restoring his composure of mind. I wondered if she had managed to lure him out from under the bed, or if they were at that very moment sandwiched between floor and bedspring.

Overcoming a momentary scruple, I put my eye to the keyhole.

Tomi was lying flat on her back, her feet planted firmly on the rug, her buttocks slightly raised, her knees wide apart so as to spring the opening between her legs. William had raised himself slightly on his arms and was working away earnestly, a frown of concentration steadily creasing his forehead. He looked like an overgrown and perturbed kewpie doll. As I watched, his movements became short and jerky, his habitually sleepy eyes opened wide as if with shock, and he came in a series of harsh, spastic thrusts.

Tomi almost literally melted into the rug, moaning in

that deep tone I knew so well, which she tried ineffectually to choke off for fear of being overheard, while her hands clawed at the olive-drab wall-to-wall carpet. Then her eyes rolled up, her back arched off the carpet, a sound like a growl escaped her; she shuddered and lay still.

I drank her cognac and then my own. I could hear Martha and Helen chattering away in the living room. Then I head Tomi's voice saying, "You dumb little freak!" and bent to take another look at the Elizabethan drama which was playing itself out in proper Darien.

Sweet William had his sister by the ankles, and as I looked he pulled her, face downwards, toward him across the rug, spreading her legs on either side of his as he did so, and forcing his short thick cock into her asshole. He held her pinned by the shoulders while she ground her face against the rug to keep from screaming with pain.

The muscles in his skinny arms stood out like cords as he held her pinned to the floor, pumping savagely and soundlessly, with a kind of grim determination while she writhed in agony. His orgasm was mercifully as quick as it was violent. He lay against her briefly, then stood up, leaving her lying on the rug.

I could hear the creak of the bed as he sat down on it, could hear him say, "I *am* a freak. That's what it's all about. Three years we've been doing it your way." (Three years! I thought. William was just fifteen last month.) "I never fucked you in the ass before, but that's what I like and when you come in here again that's what we're doing. Only let me tell you"—sneering now—"Uncle Horace sure does it better."

Tomi didn't answer. She was simply lying, very white

and very still, on the olive-drab carpet.

My sight was blurry, and all I wanted to do was sleep; I figured I was probably drunk. I went back to the living room and let myself be put to bed by Martha, who saw to it that I had the guest bedroom next to her, on the other side of the house from Tomi and Sweet William.

Chapter 6—April Concluded

Serge slept all night on the kitchen floor, soundly and well. He woke in the morning in fine spirits and could not remember any of the events of the evening. In reply to his questions about his hand, Martha, who was looking greyer and grimmer than ever, said simply that he had stumbled against the door and injured it—a fact to which the morning breeze, whistling through the broken pane, amply attested.

The only one who was in good spirits besides Serge was Helen—she, like any witch, had a secret power source from which she drew her energies. Tomi looked furtive and more nervous than ever, and Sweet William simply wasn't there at all—though he had a brilliant and vacant smile with which he greeted all circumstances of the morning. As for me, I felt totally sour: I was feeling the pangs of jealousy, and a hangover besides.

Tomi fixed me a glass of tomato juice with salt and pepper and lemon juice, anxiously trying to catch my eye as she handed it to me, and then we had some evil black coffee all round. We were indeed going sailing, and as we had risen rather early it was barely ten o'clock when we piled into the car, threw a picnic basket into the trunk, and set out for Stamford.

The Klebert's boat was a wide squat thing with a motor that they had obtained from Navy surplus. It tended to wallow, had a good bit of space below, and was particularly beloved by Serge, who delighted in taking it out on perilous and ridiculous errands, such as moving a second-hand refrigerator from Long Island to Stamford in the middle of a hurricane.

When we reached the boat basin, the day was bright and clear; a few small, high clouds were running quickly in front of the wind. Serge pointed them out.

"Probably pretty windy out there," he said with some satisfaction. "Probably choppy."

Actually, it turned out to be rather pleasant. I lay on the deck, looking up at the scudding clouds and thinking over times past.

I remembered the warm, sleepy days of last Spring: Spring on a college campus just a year ago, where all of us had been gathered together, working out the various entanglements we had invented in order to elude the great grinning demon of boredom. I had slowly introduced the people of my adolescent New York City world to the Pennsylvania college scene: plump, dark, beautiful Eva from the West Indies, with her knowing smile and her cryptic oracular statements; pale, angular Susan O'Reilley, with her sudden accesses of moodiness, her beautiful voice, her pouting, cynical mouth and innocent baby-blue eyes; and the incredibly vital, electrifying Martine, known to her friends as Petra—a veritable gold mine of the surreal and astounding in action. Petra and Tomi had become buddies at once; the bizarre in Tomi's life appealing to Petra's Spanish desire for the dramatic, the vividly colored. Eva had joined in our highly complex love-dance with her accustomed ironic grace—and Tomi and O'Reilley had fallen in love.

I recalled the week last summer spent in a cabin on the Massachusetts coast that belonged to Lee's family. We had taken the all-night "milk train" from New York to Boston, arriving in South Station at dawn, eating English muffins and coffee at the Hayes-Bickford cafeteria in the dull pink light, and then catching a bus to the coast. We got there about nine, left our suitcases in the cabin, and went immediately to the beach, eager as one always is to experience the sea.

The sea was slow and sullen, with low, grey sand dunes and no surf. The tide was out and there were mussels on the rocks, and after a halfhearted attempt to trudge across the muddy flats to the water, we gave up and turned to the more profitable business of gathering mussels. We piled a great stack of them onto a blanket and, the beach being deserted, stripped to the skin and stretched out on the sand to get as much as we could from the lukewarm New England sun. I looked over all of us with some appreciation before I lay down, taking in the muted picture we made: the curves of our bodies fitting into the lines of the dunes, the varied pinks and browns of our flesh warm against the dull sand.

It was like being in limbo: the sluggish sea and the flat

light, and I think it weighed heavily on all of us, although at the time we were unaware of it, determined as each of us was to "enjoy" the "beach." At any rate, early in the afternoon the wind came up and we seized the excuse to don our bathing suits and drag our blanket of mussels back to the cabin.

It was while she was showering in the tiny bathroom off the kitchen that Mara discovered a tick on her shoulder. There had probably been ticks in the dunes we decided, and we all gathered in the large living room in front of the fireplace to examine each other. At first we stuck rather closely to the task at hand, our bodies and the moving shadows that the firelight threw making a series of impressionistic paintings of the room.

I was examining Petra, passing my hands with great pleasure over the back of her neck and the skin behind her ears, then over her shoulders and back, feeling for the lumps that would indicate the presence of ticks. Mara was meanwhile going over my body. I had turned slightly toward her, and she, lifting one of my heavy breasts with one hand, was feeling under it with the other. As I turned I caught sight of Tomi and O'Reilley: Tomi's mouth was on one of Susan's small, pointed breasts, completely encompassing it, and her arms were around her waist, her hands clutching the two mounds of her ass. Susan's hands rested lightly on Tomi's shoulders, her head was thrown back in pleasure, her eyes shut and her mouth slightly open.

Then a warm, full mouth closed over mine, cascades of red-gold hair surrounded me, I was buried in a cloud of soft, flowery perfume. Matilda was kissing me, her arms about both me and Petra, her large, white, perfumed body pressing against the two of us. She drew back for a moment, looking into my eyes with a radiant and irrepressible smile.

"Little One," she whispered, "Oh, Little One!"—and we went down on the rug together, all three of us.

I lay on my side, my hand between Matilda's large, beautiful thighs, playing with her big clit. It felt like a bud, a perfect, closed rosebud, as it got larger and harder under my fingers. Petra lay face downwards, her head on my thighs. She was nipping at the skin, the hollow place formed by the long muscles in my legs. I turned to look at Matilda who was curled around us both like a large crescent moon, while her mouth between Petra's legs licked at cunt and asshole. Petra wrapped her legs around Matilda's head. With my head turned to the side, I tongued and bit softly at Petra's flank, at Matilda's soft hands as they clawed her sides.

My legs fell open like a sigh, and with a rush of pleasure and relief I felt Petra's strong mouth against my cunt, her warm wetness meeting my own in the gentlest and most subtle of caresses. Then her tongue came out and began playing with my clit, and I shivered and arched in pleasure as I bit down on her hips and plunged my hand deep into Matilda's moist cunt with its soft, fine-spun hair like red alchemic gold.

She was crooning, a low, pulsing sound deep in her throat playing a subtle counterpoint to Petra's deep moans. I threw my legs wider apart and turned my pelvis slightly to one side to meet Petra's mouth. As I moved, I felt Susan's cool trembling flesh against my feet. I guessed that she was still in Tomi's arms. Above my head and cut off from my sight by the wall of Matilda's body, I could hear Eva gasping as Mara murmured her name over and over. There was a huge cloud of flesh and firelight, of loving sound and soft touch, and I was floating in it. I let go. I could feel myself melting.

Explosions of lightning started in the small of my back, piercing my abdomen and shooting into my groin like liquid fire. Against my cheek Petra shuddered and came like a great, alien mammal, and my hand in Matilda's cunt ached as it was alternately squeezed by her thighs and ground by the frantic, circular movements of her pussy. The slow, heavy rhythm of Petra's orgasm cut me to the quick, and as the walls of my vagina trembled and let go in an exquisite flood of pleasure, I could hear Tomi's shout of ecstasy and her deep sobs.

I did not move for a long time. The flickering light on the ceiling slowly came back into focus. Matilda's head was on my chest, she was sucking at my breast, I could smell Petra's shit in her hair. My hand on the small of her back was sticky with her juice. Petra, asleep or blacked out, had flung herself aside, the nipples of her large breasts puckered and pointing at the ceiling, her closed eyes accented with splotches of dark shadow and a bright red flush like rouge on her high cheekbones.

Mara slipped her lithe, elongated body between Petra and me, sliding up my torso like a snake, to kiss Matilda on the back of the neck. Matilda slithered over me to meet her halfway. I passed my hand, wet with Matilda's come, over

Mara's long, slim body, anointing her. Then I turned on my side, slipping out from under the two of them, gently depositing them on the floor between Petra and me. As I did so, I felt Eva's strong, warm hands on my back.

I turned to face her, and with a hoarse, animal sound, plunged headlong into that warm, dark musky flesh, like plunging into the earth. I reveled in her full breasts with their large, blue-black nipples, her deep, round stomach, then gently parted her heavy thighs and licked at the crisp black hair of her mound, drinking in its rich, sweet odor. My tongue, with a life of its own, felt its way through the labyrinth of her hair, tipping her clitoris gently, outlining the shape of her cunt, while my hands kneaded her ass, her thighs. She came quickly, and I felt the tremors pass from her body to mine as her hand entered me from behind and set the life force on fire within me again.

Almost against my will, the trembling in my body slowly built and ebbed and built again. I was spent, exhausted by my earlier encounter. I was sure as I lay there with my head on Eva's thighs that I was too tired to come again, but the orgasm built inexorably, wracking my spine and shooting across my belly and into my groin, until finally I lost consciousness and fell into a grey heaviness between fainting and sleeping.

It was the chilliness of the room as the fire died from lack of tending that finally got us dressed, got the mussels steamed and eaten with red wine and French bread, while the fire spat pine sparks and Petra strummed a guitar. O'Reilley did not eat, but sat huddled in an armchair, her head in her arms, her long pale form curled around itself, her straight blonde hair making an aura around her, and it was then and there that Tomi fell in love with her—a love that since then had precipitated first her and then me out of the safe, closeted world of "school" and into the hectic life of the city, where we had as yet found no haven, no place in which to shape our own life form.

And now I had found the apartment, I reflected once again. My spirits had by now lifted themselves out of the doldrums into which Tomi's scene with her brother and all the sordid circumstances of her Darien life had plunged me the day before. The day was delightful, the rocking of the boat enchanting, the bright sky and high little clouds conducive to ecstasy. I had indeed found the apartment, and now it only remained for me to tell Tomi about it and get us all together in it. And see what would happen next. My head reeled at the possibilities.

We docked at the island and got our gear ashore. I was drunk with the air and the possibilities of the moment, and I immediately asked Tomi to come for a walk with me. Her conscience was still rankling over her scene of the night before, and she was anxious to please me in any way she could. We strolled along the sunny, chilly beach until we were out of earshot of the family, and then I turned to her.

"I've been waiting to tell you all weekend," I said, "that I've found a pad for us in the West Village, on Charles Street. It has two bedrooms, and a studio with a skylight, and—" I broke off when I saw her face.

"Di Prima," she said softly—almost hoarsely—not looking at me. "Forgive me. I'm not coming with you. I'm not going to live with you and O'Reilley."

At first I just didn't hear, I swept this away as an impossibility—had I not left school precisely to live with Tomi? Had I not embarked on this whole life with that in mind, so much so that the axioms and rules of the old life—of my childhood and school days—were something I could not even remember? But Tomi went on speaking, and as she did I turned to look at her small, dark ravaged face full of torment, and my eyes read in her face what my ears could not accept from her voice.

"I can't leave Martha," she was saying, improbably, pleadingly. "Please try to understand. I can't leave Martha to Serge. William is no help, I can't leave her alone with Serge. I must be what she wants me to be. What she wanted to be, and never had the chance."

She was crying now. Slowly I began to come to life. I moved my arms. I put my hands on her shoulders.

"It's your life you're talking about now, girl," I said harshly. "Your whole goddamn life."

She muttered a soft "I know it," and then, wryly, "di Prima, stop it, will you? Let's not have a goddamn scene."

I still held her by the shoulders, I still continued to gaze at her. I could not tear my eyes from that pain-racked face.

She met my eyes, and tears started down her cheeks again. "Please," she said, "please."

I drew her to me and held her close, feeling sobs shake her small body, while I rained kisses on her wet face and her crisp hair, like black fire to my lips. I, too, was shaking from head to foot.

"OK," I said when I could speak again. "OK, no scenes. You do what you have to do."

I released her, and she turned without another word and walked to the edge of the sea. She washed her face in the water while I waited, idly picking up pebbles and throwing them down again. I had no thoughts at all.

A cloud had come over the sun and it was growing chilly. Tomi returned, and we walked in silence side by side, back to the place where the family was gathered.

Martha and Helen had built a fire; hamburgers were broiling. Serge greeted us heartily, and thrust a can of beer into each of our hands. He was very happy. Like most vigorous, healthy men, at least half of his problem was simply that civilized life could not contain, or in any way use, his energies. The cool wind made him feel good. He was running around in shorts and shirt sleeves.

I made for my sweater and pulled it on, struggling to put myself together, to erase everything from my mind except proper participation in this festive event.

For the first and only time in my acquaintance with the Kleberts there was enough to eat, and nearly everyone was intent on stuffing themselves. Conversation was jovial, Martha's wit crackling like the wood she had gathered. Only Sweet William had withdrawn, sitting by himself on a rock in the water, munching a piece of celery and looking out over the horizon. Helen wrote it off for us with a joke about the trials of adolescence. I wondered if she knew how accurate she was, or had any inkling of what the trials were in this case. I hurriedly glanced at Tomi. She was pale as death, attentively lighting a cigarette, her hands shaking.

After lunch the sun put in another appearance and everyone settled down for an hour or two of rest. Martha was reading *In Country Sleep* by Dylan Thomas, which had just come out. Helen was tatting a wine-colored lace table-cloth, which she drew solemnly out of an old carpet bag. Serge had a whole book of old *New York Times* crossword puzzles. Tomi took out sketchpad and charcoal and pretended to be busy, and William—William just sat on his rock.

I withdrew a little from the others, found a more or less private hill, and stretched out in the sun. The rules of the game made it impossible for me to seek further conversation with Tomi just now: to push a point when anyone was emotionally vulnerable was "uncool." But my head was whirling with the changes that had gone down for me in the past hour, and I wanted quiet and privacy in order to put things together. Over and over I thought, "I must think about this," but no thoughts came, even the "this" did not formulate itself, and after a short while I drifted into that painful, limbo-like sleep that emotional exhaustion and confusion can bring.

I was awakened by the weight of another body on my own and a tongue in my ear. I pulled my head free and turned enough to see that Serge, complete with shorts and sunglasses, was lying on top of me.

"Please," he whispered, and for an unspeakable minute he sounded like Tomi. "Don't make any noise. They're all asleep."

His breath smelled of alcohol, and I was more than slightly repelled by his thick, older man's body. I twisted under him, managed to roll over on my stomach, and started to scramble away, intending to achieve a safe distance, sit up, and have a cool, reasonable conversation with him. He was probably drunk, and if I could get clear I could handle him easily enough. If I could just get clear—

But he was too quick, and caught me around the waist, at the same time jerking my pants, which he had unzipped while I was sleeping, down around my legs. I struggled silently to free myself, all the time thinking unbelievingly that this was rape, that I was about to be raped.

Serge somehow managed to free his rigid cock from his shorts, for I could feel it poking between my legs, looking for a way in. Suddenly his mouth was on my bare backside, I could feel that absurd moustache against my skin. And my fear and horror seemed ridiculous. This was Serge, poor silly Serge, who never got to screw his wife, and if he wanted to throw a fuck into me, why I might as well let him. It wasn't going to hurt me. Not a whole lot. Anyway, it didn't seem that I had much choice.

I stopped struggling. Serge immediately sensed my acquiescence. His hands released their vise-like grip on my shoulders, and slid under my sweater, under my blouse, and took hold of my breasts.

My legs relaxed of themselves and opened slightly to receive him. He shoved his cock in expertly. In spite of myself, pleasure began to stir in my breasts under his ministrations. I shivered bare-assed and mostly bored in the cold wind as his loins slapped against me again and again.

Then all the heavy sorrow in me turned into some crazed impersonal desire that cried out for appeasement. My cunt came reluctantly to life and I began to move with him, on my hands and knees in the grass, picking up rhythm as the energy grew.

At last I threw myself face forward on the hill, bucking and trembling in an abstract mechanical finale that even then seemed ridiculous, and Serge came with me, lying heavily across my back and panting into my ear as he shot short, hot spurts of jism into my cunt.

We lay there only for a moment, for as soon as I tensed to stir, Serge was up and off me, zipping up his fly. And before I could even turn over, his head was at the bottom of my buttocks, in the curve of my thighs, licking up his come and mine, and drying me off solicitously with a handkerchief. I was reminded abruptly of Tomi drying the mud off my feet with her panties the day before, and I spread my legs slightly to lend him better access, and pillowed my head on my arms.

When he was done I rolled over, pulled up my pants and zippered them, and then sat up and started to straighten my hair. Serge kissed me once on the cheek, in a fatherly fashion, and I patted his arm before he returned without a word to the group around the fire.

I lay there to collect myself, but that strange, brief orgasm had numbed me: driving all thoughts out of my head and almost all the sorrow out of my heart—it was still there, but in some deep place, quite out of reach, like a boulder at the bottom of a lake. The sun had gone in—for good this time, it seemed—and it was really too cold to lie there and brood, so I got up and went to find the others.

I found them packing up to go back to the boat. I helped as best I could. My head was full of cotton wool and

I was sure I walked funny. I was inexperienced at dog-fashion fucking and had probably torn the skin of my cunt a little. The tight jeans didn't help any. Tomi glanced at me quizzically once or twice, but I managed to avoid her eyes.

We had no sooner set out than it began to blow. A real storm, a lulu of a storm, had come up. The boat rocked and wallowed, the rain came down, and nearly everyone went down into the cabin. As for me, I knew I couldn't face close scrutiny by either Tomi or Martha, so I climbed up onto the roof of the cabin and sat there hanging on with both hands and looking at the sky.

Lightning broke again and again, thunder crashed. Serge stood at the helm, soaked to the skin, singing at the top of his voice. His wet, clinging shorts revealed that he had another erection.

It was as if the weather and I were in complete agreement. I sat there, drinking it in, feeling for the first time in my life how much turbulence I could contain in quiet, what endurance was, being cleansed by the purity, the pure fury of the elements. Finally Serge became aware that I was there and, either out of concern for me or embarrassment over the events of the day, ordered me below, saying he could not be responsible if I were washed overboard.

In the cabin they were all seasick; the roof was leaking. Martha sat holding a blanket like a tent over Sweet William who, huddled in fetal position, was trying to sleep. Helen and Tomi were trying to play cards, but after a while they gave that up and just sat there, Tomi, pale as death, making small noncommittal grunts in answer to Helen's incessant chatter.

A picture flashed into my mind from a storehouse of memory, a story Tomi had told me about a music teacher she had had a crush on as a child of twelve. How the woman had finally seduced her one day under the walnut tree in front of the house. How Martha had seen them and threatened Tomi with reform school and the woman with the police if she ever came to the house again. Now, as I thought of that story, they all three appeared in my head in Victorian dress: Tomi and her friend standing formally, almost classically, under the tree, Martha corseted and in a high ruff standing in the doorway of the house. Rather like Henry James, I thought. They think they're Fitzgerald, but they're like a mean Henry James. . . .

There was no air in the cabin, and it was stifling hot. I picked up *In Country Sleep*, and read by the light of a flashlight. "Never and never my girl riding far and near . . ."

We got there, though I don't know how, docking in Stamford finally, and by then I knew that I couldn't face another night of it, that I had to go somewhere, anywhere, out of there, out of that thick air, those woven lives. I knew that once I got away I would find the means to stay away, that I would not be seeing Tomi again.

"Yes," she said, "you can catch the 9:20, but I thought you were coming back with us."

I mumbled something about having just remembered some job or other that I would have to get to in the morning, some lame excuse, while Martha scrutinized me with those ultra-clear grey eyes.

"All right then, we'll leave you at the station," she said

with more kindness than I had ever heard from her. "Serge can bring in your suitcase when he goes to the city to work tomorrow."

Tomi said nothing, but when we piled into the car she contrived to sit next to me. I was aware of the flesh of her thigh against mine, the understated harshness of her breathing. We rode in silence, and when I got out Tomi got out with me, to walk with me to the ticket booth and get me on the right platform. It was still raining softly.

"Di Prima," said Tomi, "di Prima, talk to me."

"What is there to say?" I asked her. "You know what you're giving up."

I meant O'Reilley, but I meant light and freedom, air and laughter, the outside world—outside of the stuffy incestuous atmosphere of her "family life." I meant drawing tables in high white rooms, nights at the ballet or at some exotic restaurant, or simply wandering, exploring the neon streets. And mostly I meant laughter, the silliness and glee unscrutinized, one's blood running strong and red in one's own veins, not drawn to feed the uneradicable grief of the preceding generation.

"I'll forget her," said Tomi, meaning O'Reilley. "I can't do it to Martha."

We were mercifully in shadow, and I took and kissed those small, beautiful hands again and again, before I turned and walked to the platform without looking back.

And at last my tears fell, as the rain fell, endlessly, hopelessly, as I watched the old black Chrysler pull out and turn toward the Darien woods, carrying the small creature I loved better than anything else in the world.

Chapter 7—
Some Ways to Make a Living

"You're gonna have to move in a little closer there, Joe. Put your mouth right on her for this one. You're OK, Bob. OK, Diane, pull up your left knee just a little now, now lift your chin, throw your head back a bit more. Wet you lips."

A soft, almost polite mouth closed over my breast, a large black hand took hold of my naked waist. I pulled my left knee up slightly, threw my head back, and held still. Click. A flood of inordinately bright light played over the three of us. Click. This time the slower click of a camera shutter, repeated three or four times.

"OK, gang, that's it."

The tableau came to life. Bob raised his head from between my legs, Joe took his mouth off my right breast, and we all stood up. And laughed, to break the tension, the strange sexual closeness that had already taken hold of us.

"Whew!" said Bob. "Whew-eee! Well, at least you got a nice pussy, honey. Some white pussy sure does smell foul."

"Why, thank you, Bob," I said, laughing. I slid a sister-ly arm around his waist for a minute, before I turned away to slip on my kimono.

We were in a loft that existed as lofts existed only in New York City, and only in the New York of the nineteen-fifties. A huge, grey, dusty space, suspended, hung in mid-air just to the east of Union Square—a space as quiet and black and lonely as the desert, existing in its own peculiar dimension of silence, to which no one could gain access without the total cooperation of the inhabitant.

This particular loft belonged to one Duncan Sinclair, photographer and part-time pornographer. Duncan was a suave, genial black man in his mid-thirties. Now he handed beers round to all of us, and we sat around, joking and talk-ing easily about nothing at all.

Joe was a painter, in that vivid, expressionistic school of black East Coast painting that has never been seen or heard of there—though it has in Europe—because it is far too vital and alive (and heterosexual) for any East Coast art gallery. He was running down a recipe for poor food for me: something called "hopping john," made of brown rice and kidney beans with ham hocks.

Bob was a bartender at a downtown Fifth Avenue bar. He was tall and beautiful and very black, and he did these gigs by day to pick up a little extra money.

I sat there, tired and vaguely hungry, half listening as the three talked, and half letting my thoughts roam wher-ever they would.

It was just a few weeks since I had moved into the apartment on the Lower East Side that I had found for myself after Tomi had decided not to join me. Without her, the Village studio I had found for us had somehow lost its point, and besides it was way too expensive. Instead I had taken a tiny "renovated" two and a half rooms, on Avenue A and Fifth Street. I had a forward-looking landlord, an ancient rabbi who had decided, way back then, that the East Side was to become the "new Village" and he had bought up a few tenements, cut down the apartments to appropriately small sizes, and was hoping to rent them to impoverished young people who thought as he did, or who simply wanted a haven, any haven they could afford, within walking distance of the bars, coffee shops and book stores.

I was the only one he had found so far. Whenever I entered or left the smelly hall of that sad building, whose exterior bravely sported a new coat of grey paint, I ran the gauntlet of the small suspicious eyes of literally hundreds of Polish, Ukrainian, and Hungarian women, who could not tell what I was doing in their midst, but did not like it, did not like it at all.

Walking down Fifth Street from Avenue A, I first passed an incredibly odoriferous funeral parlor, then a small meat-packing concern whose sidewalk was perpetually stained and greasy from sausage fat, and then an equally rank bar, where I daily experienced the scrutiny and catcalls of the lewd, sex-starved men who belonged to the aforementioned narrow-eyed women. Proposals were there made to me, desperations held out, hopes whispered, that were somehow lower and more loathsome than anything I have encountered anywhere since.

After paying the rent, the month's deposit, the one-month agency fee, the gas and electric deposit, and the telephone deposit, and purchasing such bare necessities as a frying pan and a blanket, I found myself totally broke, and began to look around anxiously for a way to earn a living. On a crosstown bus I had found a discarded copy of *Show Business*, and there found an ad for "sexy girl models," which offered an enticing ten dollars an hour and up. I had my doubts about whether or not I qualified, but I was amply filling out my C-cup brassieres, and my waist was the prescribed ten inches smaller than my bust and hip line, which came to within an inch of being the same size, and so, having no information to go on except a phone number, I decided to give it a try.

Two days and three phone calls later, I found myself in the office of one Gay Faye, while he regarded me sagely.

"Stand up again, dear, will you?" he had said abruptly. "Now, turn around, let me see you from the side. Well, it's worth a try, I guess. Raise your skirt, will you, let me see your legs."

I bent to do so, hoisting my skirt to within half an inch of my pussy, wondering what he would propose next.

"Look," I said, "I'm not shy. Why not just have me undress, and see if I'll do or not?"

"I'm coming to that, dear," said Gay with a grimace. "I'm coming to that. I like to work up to it slowly. Take off your skirt and blouse now, let me see your undies. My God, what dowdy lingerie. I hope you brought something better with you."

"Yes," I said, "I brought a couple of garter belts and stockings and some sheer panties and a black lace bra."

"Well, that's a start, anyway," said he, lighting a Du Maurier. "Now take off your underwear."

I did, and he said, "Now put your panties back on and take them off again, only this time turn your back to me while you do it."

I obeyed, feeling rather like a trained seal in a circus, while he regarded my ass, first from one side and then the other.

"Not bad," said Mr. Faye. "You really look much pudgier in those clothes than you actually are. Women never *will* learn to dress." He perched his brittle and angular self on the edge of the desk. "Do you want to start today?"

"Sure," said I. "Why not? I mean, I'd like to, very much." I felt as if I had started already.

"Good," he said. "Then put that robe on, will you? And you might as well go into the kitchen and fix yourself some coffee. We can't start till the marks go away."

"Marks?" I said.

"Red line under your breasts from your bra," he said with some relish. "Almost looks like a welt. Small crease on your stomach from the elastic of your underpants."

"True," I said, though I had never thought of it before. I felt like the heroine in an S-and-M novel.

I put on the robe, a thirties imitation of a black silk kimono, embroidered with the loudest and most obnoxious of peonies, and wandered off in the direction he had indicated to see if I could indeed make some coffee.

Mr. Gay Faye was as gay as his name. He absolutely hated the female form, and devoted the entire practice of his art to contorting, obscuring and confusing it by any means possible. The productions of his camera, reproduced in full color by the tens of thousands, passed as sexy, were glued onto calendars and hung in garages and dens all over America. They kept him and the ex-weight lifter who kept house and lived with him in the comfort they so amply deserved.

We began with a series of nude shots, me kneeling and sitting back on my haunches, my hands in my long hair and my head turned to the side—trying to look coy, or what I thought was coy, which I later altered to what I thought Gay Faye would think was coy. A whole series of back shots, me leaning over an armchair, chin propped in my hands, looking bored. A shot of me bending over, looking out through my legs.

"I'm very limited," complained Gay, "because of your *hair*. Look, if we do a lot of this, would you consider shaving your pubic hair?"

I got a prickly, itchy feeling between my legs at the very thought, and I frowned—what I hoped was thoughtfully.

"I don't know," I said. "Depends on how much work there is."

"Certainly not," is what I was thinking. "Life is hard enough."

I strode about in a garter belt and stockings and high-heeled shoes. Stood in a sheer nightie against a window, legs spread apart, arms stretched straight up. Curled up on a bearskin, nude again, with Gay's obnoxious little Chihuahua in my lap, covering the offending hair. Stood by Gay's table with its lace tablecloth in a maid's cap and apron and the eternal high heels, holding a silver tray with a silver tea service just below my bare boobs. Stepped out of the shower dripping wet, in lace shower cap and scanty towel, one long strand of red hair clinging wetly to my breast and curling around the nipple.

We stopped, exhausted. Warren the weight lifter went out for hero sandwiches and containers of coffee. Then I got dressed and we called it a day.

I worked for Gay two or three times more. And then on one occasion Duncan dropped in to do some shooting on the bearskin rug, and asked me if I'd work for him.

"The work is a little different," he said. "More—uh—realistic. But the pay is better—I'll give you twenty-five dollars an hour."

"Great," I said. (My rent was forty-five dollars a month.) "When do you want to start?" I figured he meant pornography, but had already decided that real, honest-to-god pornography would not be half as obscene as the stuff I was doing for Gay.

There had followed a series of these ultra-polite sessions. Most of the porn was faked, and what little was not was performed with a combination of courtesy and know-how that left me curious as to what the follow-up would be like.

Duncan had offered me a permanent job as his secretary and receptionist in addition to the shooting sessions, the only stipulation being that I work—type, answer the phone, etc.—entirely in the nude. I declined, because, as I explained to him, I figured that I was making more than enough money and didn't want to tie myself up with a regular job. Duncan chortled endlessly at the idea that he had offered me a "regular job," and we continued to get together a couple of times a week for shooting sessions.

Now, just as I was about to get dressed to go home, Bob turned to me, and I could see that, whatever it was that he had on his mind, he had been mulling it over for some time.

"Say, listen, Diane, I wonder if you would do me a favor. I never told you this, but I have a collection—I've been collecting photographs of cunts for some time now. I guess I have over three thousand cunts by this time: white ones, black ones, chink cunts, all kinds. I even have Joan Crawford's cunt. So I was wondering—I was wondering would you let Duncan take a picture of your pussy. You don't have to do anything, nobody else in the picture, just lie there, just you lie back with your legs open and let him take a picture of your pussy."

"Sure," I said. "Why not?" I turned to Duncan. "You want to do that now?"

"If you're not too tired," said Duncan. "I'm still set up."

I lay back on the couch, Joe got up and switched on the floodlights, Bob watched, impassively drinking his beer while Duncan clicked his camera, made a few adjustments of the lens, moved me slightly and clicked it again.

"I tried two different openings," he said to Bob, and laughed uproariously at his own pun. "We'll see which comes out better."

"Hey, listen, thanks a lot," Bob said as I started to get dressed.

"Oh, it was nothing," I told him truthfully enough. "I'd

sure like to see your collection sometime."

"Anytime you want," said Bob. "Maybe," he added hopefully, "when Duncan gets this developed you could sign it for me."

"Sure," I said, "I'll come up to your place and sign it."

The telephone was ringing when I got back to the apartment. It was Petra, calling from the mysterious "downtown" where she worked.

"Dearie, do you want to pick up some money? I have a little job for you."

"Sure," I said. "Anything short of streetwalking."

"There's a fellow in my office who needs a correspondent for his divorce case. You don't have to do anything—I mean he won't molest you or—"

"You mean I don't have to fuck him."

"Right, dearie, nothing like that, you just have to be seen—oh, it's very complicated—do you want to do it? I'll give you his phone number."

"I guess so," I said, "near as I can make out."

Next day found me in a taxi, speeding up Fifth Avenue toward the nineties. Doormen approached cautiously. I spoke the password and they became gracious. Elevators opened and closed silently. I walked on plush carpets down long, spooky halls.

"Mr. Vandenberg vill be right dere," the maid said in her almost-Swedish, and left me in a room full of uncomfortable chairs, flowers, and even more uncomfortable Art. Then Mr. Vandenberg appeared and I suddenly understood my environment.

We introduced ourselves and shook hands. He would not meet my eyes.

"I'll take very little of your time, Miss di Prima," he said dolefully. "If you will kindly step this way." A cultured Berlin accent.

We walked into a dimly lit bedroom, heavy draperies forming a thirties-movies arch over the high windows. I pulled them aside a trifle and looked out. Central Park stretched below us, full of sunshine, a reminder of another, greener planet.

Mr. Vandenberg suddenly remembered the duties of a host. "Would you like a drink?"

"No, I don't think so," I said. "Why don't you just tell me what it is I have to do."

He ran it down.

"Fine," I said. "Now, Mr. Vandenberg, I hesitate to bring up so delicate a subject, but Miss Vegas told me that remuneration for this—service—was to be—"

"One hundred dollars," he said, looking away sadly. "Will that do?"

"Yes," I said. "I think so. Can you pay me half of it in advance?"

Mr. Vandenberg reached for his wallet and drew out a hundred-dollar bill.

"I did not anticipate this request of yours, Miss di Prima, and I have nothing smaller. Do let me pay you in full now; it will be less embarrassing. We might find it difficult to do business in the presence of my wife's friends."

"Thank you," I said, "and while you're at it, you'd better call me Diane, don't you think? I mean, if you're supposed to know me that well, and all." It was hard to tell for sure in the dim light of the bedroom, but I could almost swear he was blushing.

"Thank you, Diane," he said, as gallantly as possible. "Please call me Wolfgang." He looked at his watch. "My wife and her friends should be here in exactly ten minutes, so if you would be so kind as to undress . . ."

"Completely?"

"If you do not seriously object, it would be better if you undressed completely." There was almost the suggestion of a bow, and he left the room.

I took off all my clothes, folded them, and placed them in an unobtrusive pile on the chair. Then I considered, took one stocking out of the pile, and dangled it conspicuously over the side of the chair, which I moved so that it was quite close to the bed—close enough so that it would, I figured, get in the photographs. I threw my brassiere on the floor. After all, I thought, we might as well have a dash, just a dash, of realism about all this.

Mr. Vandenberg came out of his dressing room in a bathrobe. He looked more pained than ever. His eye rested for a moment on the bra and stocking, but he said nothing about them. Then he opened the draperies and flipped a switch that controlled an indirect light right over the bed.

"You must excuse me," he said, "but they will need enough light to take pictures."

"Of course," I mumbled, nestling into the incredibly fine sheets, thinking how much I would like a nap.

"Do you mind," he asked, "if I drink? I feel the need of something to quiet my nerves."

"Not at all," I told him. "Go right ahead."

He rang for the Swedish maid and she appeared immediately with a tall glass of Scotch on the rocks. He looked down into it sadly.

"I can't tell you how much my wife and I appreciate this, Miss di—uh—Diane. The divorce laws in this state are so stringent—so very stringent."

He shook his head, ran his hands through his toupee, took a swallow of Scotch. Then he looked at his watch again, and sat down abruptly on the edge of the bed.

"Excuse me," he said, "but we must look more lover-like."

He took the covers down from my shoulders and uncovered one breast. He arranged my hair slightly on the pillow and, bending close over me, took one of my hands in both of his.

The door opened as if on cue. A handsome woman of about forty stood in the doorway. Three other people stood behind her. She stood as if shocked for a moment, then turned to the nearest of them.

"Oh," she said, in the measured, distinct tones of a bad actress. "Do you see that?"

"What?" asked the person addressed, a thin, nervous young man in a peach-colored suit.

"That woman and Wolfgang, in *my* bed!"

Now this was scarcely accurate, but they all declared that they *did* see it. They all piled into the room, the last of the young men bearing a camera. He used it. Wolfgang, who had not moved all this time, now turned his profile to the camera. Friend took another picture. Wolfgang said,

"Simone, my dear, I am sorry about this." Simone put her handkerchief to her face. Simone put away her handkerchief. Simone put her hand on Wolfgang's shoulder. She gazed at me soulfully.

"You are invited to stay for lunch," she said to me.

"Thank you," I said.

Everyone piled out of the room again, and I got up and started to get dressed, tucking the crisp hundred-dollar bill deep in my pocket, and wondering at the ways of the Law.

Chapter 8—City Spring

My pad gradually filled up, as pads generally do. A collection of oddments—souls with no home and no particular merits—about whom the most I could say was that they were not boring, slept on the floor, or in the big double bed with me. The bed would hold up to four of us comfortably, and out of this fact grew nuances of relationship most delicate in their shading. I remember that at one point there were the following souls in and about the house: Red-haired Lauren, Young Jack, Henry with the Big Ears, and Runaway Julie.

Red-haired Lauren was a particularly degenerate-looking (and acting) young man in his mid-twenties, who delighted in collecting the youngest available specimens of the human race and experimenting on them—physically and psychologically. I never let him sleep in my bed. He turned my stomach. However, he stayed in the pad for the better part of a month because he was a friend of Young Jack.

Young Jack was very beautiful, with large blue-green

eyes, open gentle manner, big strong hands, and a good body. He was a good fuck and liked to fuck a lot, and he was fifteen years old. I remember that the night I found out his age I went through a lot of changes; I was eighteen, nearly nineteen—was I robbing the cradle? But decided I couldn't care less, and returned to the business at hand. I got very fond of Jack—he gave me a chance to thoroughly exercise both my sexual and maternal skills, a chance that, especially at eighteen, is rarely come on in this world.

It was as if he had been born for fucking. I still remember how he rode me, eager and beatific, his fine mouth and well-made cock that filled me so well, touched me so deep, and sent a dark fire out from my stomach and loins to sweep through my limbs and to the roots of my hair. Or how he would kneel, one knee on each side of my head, and go down on me, his salty cock filling my mouth, the musty smell of his hair, his ass, in my nostrils, the two of us one cosmic geometric form as we strained together in the dark, and often as not some other young creature curled up asleep beside us, or stirring half-sleepily awake, licking and kissing breast and side and ass of one or the other of us, indiscriminately loving whoever, whatever came within his or her range.

One night when Young Jack and I arrived back home from a pointless and joyous springtime jaunt to the Village, we found Lauren sitting in the hall by the door—I had given him a key—hovering, half-crouching over a skinny pouting gamine complete with pixie haircut and big brown eyes. Her clothes proclaimed her middle-class Queens; her fright declared her new to the scene. I let them in, and so

Runaway Julie was added to the menage. She slept in the bed with me and Jack and joined our preliminary games, sometimes allowing me to lead her almost to the edge of a quick little panting orgasm—but Runaway Julie didn't put out. This was considered a challenge by the ego-ridden Lauren, and he brought to bear all of his enormous (he thought) powers of seduction: introducing her to the various haunts in the Village, reading Freud aloud to her, filling her head with his own garbled philosophy—a kind of mixture of Aleister Crowley and Karl Marx—but he got nowhere at all. Julie confined herself to crushes, and confined her crushes to those Village faggots whose homosexuality was so total that she could not possibly feel the slightest threat in their presence. With them she was her playful, total self—a child among children.

I don't know how or when Henry with the Big Ears arrived. He was a mumbling, vague, gentle soul, and a mathematical genius—a drop-out from the Electronics Research Lab at Columbia University. His only loves were cocaine and Indian philosophy, and he indulged both constantly, unobtrusively occupying an empty corner, a small person of uncertain age in his nondescript rags. We all loved him—anyone would have loved him once they noticed that he was there. Henry slept wherever he fell out—bed or floor was all one to him—he easily wrapped himself around any of us, and easily fell asleep to the rocking rhythms of our lovemaking.

Henry was little, but well-hung, with a long, slender, well-formed cock and a supple body. When he took cocaine his staying power was enormous. He could—and occasionally did—literally fuck for hours, past orgasm and the possibility of orgasm, to the point of madness. I liked to keep him waiting, feeling his cock grow hard against my flank while I fucked Young Jack to sleep, angelically and joyously. Then I would turn on my side, slipping softly out from under Jack's pretty body with its smooth skin and the baby fat still on his thighs and face—turn on my side to Henry, who would be waiting for me with a grin on his face and his long dick in his hand.

I would throw one leg over him, pressing him close to me with my heel in the small of his back, and the whole of his long supple cock would slide into me easily—my cunt still slippery from my come and Jack's—and we would rock and sway together endlessly through a whole spectrum of pleasure while Young Jack and Julie slept oblivious on either side of us.

And so the days passed easily—it was a cool, beautiful Spring and the East Side was blooming: pads like my own were beginning to spring up here and there, one on Seventh Street, one on East Twelfth. Rienzi's, a new coffee shop specifically for the "young Bohemian crowd," had opened up on MacDougal Street: Mafia-run, like the Italian espresso joints, it did not cater to the usual Mafia clientele. We all sat there in the long afternoons, reading and making each other's acquaintance, nursing twenty-five cent cups of espresso for hours, and drawing pictures on paper napkins. Intoxicated by the stories of our youth, by *Jean-Christophe* and *La Bohéme*, we thought to play a similar game. We almost carried it off.

There was the day Little John burst into our house—someone had given him our address and he was sick and needing a place to stay. We put him to bed with us and watched horrified as his fever rose from a hundred and three to a hundred and five and a half. He tossed and turned all night delirious, while we all drank cups of coffee and played chess, unable to sleep. The next day I paid a visit to a good friend, and older guy named Glenn, who was a longshoreman with a line into almost any drug one could need or desire. I got a handful of seconal and administered them two at a time to the still-delirious John. He fell asleep. We all fell out, exhausted. And woke when his pills wore off and his ravings began again, and gave him two more pills. Next day red bumps on his neck and groin announced, we decided (having seen *Forever Amber*) that he had the bubonic plague. We continued to sleep beside him. We continued to give him pills for two more days and nights, as everyone's nerves wore thin. On the third morning, Little John woke seemingly lucid, and announced cryptically, "If I read Baudelaire this morning, I'm going to vomit." "So *nu?*" I thought in New York Yiddish exasperation, and went out. When I returned in the afternoon, there was John, sitting hale and hearty at the kitchen table. "I read Baudelaire," he grinned, "and I vomited."

Or there was the afternoon that I sat with O'Reilley at Rienzi's sipping jasmine tea and reading *Journey to the East*, feeling for all the world like a Lady Writer, when up to our table wandered Big Jack, a mulatto boy about six-foot-six with a glazed look in his eyes. He took his two hands out of his pockets, whereupon we saw his wrists were cut, rather badly and jaggedly. "My pockets," he announced somewhat sadly, "are full of blood." "I'll bet they are," I said. We took him outside, made tourniquets of napkins from Rienzi's twisted about with a pencil, and then finally made bandages of more napkins and sent him on his way. But he didn't go far. We were eating in Minetta's Tavern on the corner an hour or two later when he wandered in lugubriously calling our names. Fed him our soup, took him home. Runaway Julie's remark: "I think I'm taking it very well for my first suicide." Gave him the sleeping pills left over from Little John's plague. He fell asleep between me and Henry. Julie slept on the floor because, as she said, "I don't want to wake up in the morning next to a corpse." Two days and three suicide attempts later, he seemed somewhat put together. We filled him full of leftover take-home sweet-and-sour Chinese food, sold the pawn tickets for our various possessions and bought him a ticket. Big Jack got on a bus and went back to his people in Worcester, Massachusetts.

The days got longer. About as long as they get. The changes began, summer changes in New York. Young Jack left for a summer stock job someplace in Indiana. Lauren found a chick his own age with a job, who wanted her own private magician, and he moved in with her. Henry with the Big Ears went off to build a corrugated tin shack on the Brooklyn mud flats together with two dropped-out physicists from MIT. And Runaway Julie went home to Forest Hills. O'Reilley and I lingered on in the pad, eating Pepperidge Farm bread and *bleu* cheese sandwiches in memory of Tomi, and writing in large grey notebooks.

Then one evening I was walking crosstown to meet her in the Cafe Montmartre (favorite bar of the season, filled with calypso singers with gold earrings and conga drums, and messianic painters with curly, dirty beards who drank and fucked extravagantly). I had just been job-hunting, and so I trudged along in a blue skirt and blue high heels, half hoping to break them, or at least wear them down faster. A car pulled up alongside me and kept pace with my slow walk, a voice I half-knew called my name and, on my turning to answer, about three voices cried, "Do you want to go to the country?"

To one who lives in New York City, the country is the country. It is all one whether you mean the Adirondacks or the Arizona desert. The country is simply Not-The-City. It means you can see the sky, and probably something green, and maybe the stars at night. Everyone in New York City always wants to go to the country, is bored to death all the while they are there, drinks as much as possible, and expresses great regret on returning to the city. Of course I wanted to go to the country. I hopped right into the car, stockings and high heels and all, squeezed in between a skinny blonde girl in a Navajo skirt and a young boy with a banjo, and off we went.

We arrived after dark somewhere on a hill not far from the Hudson. A hill full of bonfires, soft sounds of guitars. Hard to say how many people, maybe about two hundred, scattered in small groups over the landscape.

I found my way to a fire, blanketless and chilly, and sat still to hear a warm, untrained voice singing "Spanish Is a

Loving Tongue." There was a good, rich smell on the breeze which I recognized as pot—I'd been around it often enough, though I'd never had any. Then a fat, loosely rolled joint came into my hands and I took a drag on it.

Wind soft and balmy, slightly moist and smelling of green things. Young faces in the firelight, young bodies casting long shadows. Young Bill Thompson stopped singing for a minute and threw me a blanket. "You must be cold." Everyone huddled in twos and threes in their jeans under Indian blankets, afghans, open sleeping bags.

The music went on: "The south coast is a wild coast and lonely." Moon coming up on the wane, hardly any light from the pallid thing in the sky.

The grass went around, again and again. I began to get what I guessed was "stoned." A clear, beautiful focusing-in on each and every person and thing. Hands intensely aware of texture feeling grass and pebbles. Warm total contentment and immobility. I searched out the shadowy faces, breathed deep, looked at the dull moon through the trees.

The wind died. People began to fall asleep. Then the music stopped. I looked up to see Billy's face, sculptured in the firelight, close to my own. With no thought, my arms went around him and drew him down beside me onto the blanket. With no thought, I undid the layers of clothing that kept us apart. Fine young body, solidly there, beautifully untense but eager. Fine golden glow from the fire, reflected by his flesh, reflected flickering with shadows, fine hairs catching the light, turning golden.

And lying on my side, my mouth not for one moment leaving his, I took him into me, took his large, red-gold cock, and we made love under the stars. Made love in the firelight, surrounded with the warmth, the other couples fucking or sleeping, delightfully hewn and sculpted by the flame. Made love, and made love again, smell and touch alive as never before, all our skin one flaming organ of touch.

And fell asleep, his large hand on my hip, his coat over us both, a warm wind stroking our hair.

I awoke to the blue light of dawn, a few squeaky birds calling to each other over my head, an ant walking on my arm. I moved one foot on the blanket and pulled it back again: except where it had been kept dry by the warmth of our bodies the blanket was clammy with dew.

I raised my head and looked at the sleeping boy beside me, so different in this blue light than he had seemed in the jewelled darkness of the firelight. A good face: big nose, wide cheekbones; strange to see the white color of his flesh and mine, so deeply imprinted in my memory was our golden-glowing skin. Then he opened his eyes, deep deep brown and luminous, and grinned a friendly, happy good morning and rolled over on top of me . . .

Morning was soft talk and more dope, as the young sleepy people woke up in twos and threes and greeted each other and the day. The young men stomped about in blue jeans and boots, sharing cigarettes and finding places behind the trees to piss, while the girls sat, still half inside their sleeping bags, pulling on sweaters and peasant skirts and braiding their long hair.

Then the good smell of food drifted over the hill to us and we wandered toward it. Right near the small farmhouse, someone had built a large fire and on it sat a cauldron of bubbling stew. Billy's father, Big Bill, stood over it, stirring and tasting. He was a tall, spare, hawk-faced man in his forties, very handsome and very black-Irish.

After breakfast people scattered to walk, to look at the hills, to go see the Hudson, only a couple of miles away. Billy and I fell in with a bunch of kids who were going fishing. A short bumpy car ride took us to a weird, shaky wooden pier thrusting out into the river, where we sat down, got stoned, and watched the shadows of the clouds on the mountains, incidentally dangling some fishing line into the water.

Things bit, and kept biting. They were all eels. Eels were about the only thing still living in that filthy water. Still, they were a bounty. We pulled them up, watched them thrash and flop around, dying, and when we left we toted them all along with us in a pillowcase.

We found a quiet piece of woods and, while Billy built a fire, I cleaned the eels with his knife, grateful to my Brooklyn Italian upbringing that had made the process familiar. Then we improvised a kind of grill out of green willow and birch branches and grilled them quickly. We ate sitting on our heels in the wet moss, and washed the fish down with cheap wine that one of the guys produced from his back pocket. It was delicious.

By the time we made it back to the campsite, everyone had gathered around one big fire. The music was already happening: Eric's banjo and Bob's twelve-string guitar were in full swing, and two or three people had started drumming. I lay down next to Billy, and he began to sing, and after a while there were many people singing, and a bass guitar got going, and the stars came out, and Big Bill came and joined us, grinning quietly in the dark.

Chapter 9—Country Spring

It was a long time before I got back to the city. On Sunday night, when everyone was getting ready to split, Billy asked me to stay on for a while and live with him, and I said I would. I had never lived in the country before, never really lived in a place that was growing its own vegetables, and I wanted to know what that felt like. And besides Billy and I dug making it together, and I was writing, and so there was no reason to go anywhere else. Next day I sawed the high heels off my shoes, and borrowed a pair of Billy's big, baggy jeans, which I tied with a rope around my middle to keep them on, and began to live in the country.

Big Bill gave us a small, empty house on the place, just for the two of us, and that blew my mind, because up till then practically my whole relationship with the older generation had been one of lies and avoidance. But Big Bill was a thirties Red, and a staunch believer in "free love," and he totally approved of our scene and us, and thought we were good for each other—besides, he dug having me around.

He and Billy had a summer job working on the state highway, and they would leave very early in the morning and come back about five. I would get up with Billy and go over to the kitchen in the big house, where I would get the coffee going, fry a bunch of home-fries, and make eggs and oatmeal for the men. After they split for work I would slowly get dressed, clean up the house and our shack, weed the garden a little, read, write, walk, listen to Big Bill's short-wave radio. The time passed very quickly, and then it was time to boil the potatoes—each of them ate three potatoes at supper, and you had to boil another two apiece for home-fries next morning. While the potatoes were cooking, I would go out to the garden and look at the vegetables, trying to determine what was ripe enough for dinner, pulling up a tentative beet or carrot to see if it was ready. I had never encountered growing vegetables in any quantity before—our victory garden in Brooklyn when I was a kid had sported nothing but plum tomatoes for tomato sauce—and half the time I wasn't sure what it was that was growing. I made a few outrageous mistakes, but mostly stuck to things I recognized—that looked approximately as big, and about the same color, as when I bought them in stores in the city—and once in a while I asked Big Bill about something I didn't recognize; I didn't like to do this much, because every one of my questions seemed to call forth a burst of (to me) totally unwarranted mirth.

Besides Big Bill and Billy, Little John (who had formerly had the bubonic plague) was staying at the place, and I found I really dug being woman to the three men, cleaning and mending and cooking for them. Looking back on it now, I think it was because they were all working so hard that they came home relaxed and easy, pleased with the food, pleased with the house, delighted to have a woman around at all.

Billy and I dug making it in the morning. We would often wake up before it was light, thrown back to the surface from the deep place of our sleep by our hunger for each other, a hunger which had fed all night long on the brushing and gentle touch of flesh on flesh as we dreamed.

Our bed was under the window, and when I woke first I would look at the sky to see if the morning star was out. If it was, I would reach out and touch the boy beside me, the smooth flesh of stomach, dip of navel as he lay on his side, my hand slipping over his wide chest, fingers touching his lips which were half-open to his breathing. He would turn toward me, still asleep, and I would kiss him, a slight trembling in my body which was desire, and sleepiness, and the chill of the early morning dampness.

Then we would waken, large warm hands would take hold of me, would slip under the small of my back and raise me closer to him. We would explore each other with slow, swimming gestures, the gestures of sleep, our dreams still upon our eyes, the flavor of them filling each other's mouths as we kissed, long and endlessly.

Billy's legs were so beautiful, I loved to run my hands over his thighs, to slip my hand between them, to feel his smooth, muscled ass. Then, slowly, the trembling would stop as I grew warm, as I ceased to tense my body against desire, and I would lie moist and open, full in my very hunger, and he would enter me. We would move together in

101

the semi-darkness, slow and long, savoring our pleasure, building it slowly, slowly, lying sometimes at right angles to one another, sometimes parallel and side by side, and sometimes, briefly, Billy would be on me, or I on him.

At last his excitement would grow, he would begin pumping faster and faster, would sit up and pull me to a sitting position, impaled on his long, thick cock, so that I sat full on him, with my legs wrapped around him, my arms around his neck, and looking full into his eyes as I moved up and down on his lap, aided by the movement of his thighs, I would come, falling forward against his chest while he moaned and jerked, filling me with the juices of his being.

Then he would lie back, his arms around me, his cock still in me, and we would lie together motionless while I smelled the smells of the old house, the damp, rotting wood and mouldy earth smells, and the light came slowly into the room.

And often as not as we lay there, his limp, wet cock still inside me, I would feel it stir and begin to come to life again, and I would begin to stroke and smooth his large, beautiful balls. His prick would slip out of me, only half-hard, and I would close my mouth over it; the musky taste of my own come and the salty, slightly bitter taste of his would mingle in my mouth, the point of my tongue would seek out the small opening of his prick, my fingers on his asshole and the underside of his balls would stir him back to desire.

Then he would turn me over, and slip his wet, slippery cock into my ass and his fingers into my cunt so that I was completely filled with him, pressed against the cool, musty-smelling mattress, my hands thrown over my head or reaching back to stroke and fondle him. And he would nip and nuzzle at my neck and back, moaning great, boyish, animal moans, while I felt as if I would literally explode with the fullness, the total submergence of my being in his incredible male desire. I would be set quivering in every fibre of my flesh, and would cry out in the still morning, while I came again in an endless spasm of release which left me hollow, concave and empty, white light like lightning exploding in my brain.

Fuck The Pill: A Digression

On his first trip to town, Billy had embarrassedly purchased some Trojans, and he used them on our first night in our cottage—and, at my insistence, never used them again. I understood and appreciated the thought behind them, but they were a drag. Up to that time, I had never used any contraceptives at all. In fact, for the first few years of my running around town I never used anything to avoid pregnancy, and never once got pregnant. Some kind of youthful charisma kept the thing going.*

The one time I thought I was knocked up, two weeks late with my period, I took a long walk in the broiling sun (it was a July) with a red-haired maniac junkie named Ambrose, down along West Street, past the trucks and the

---

*N.B. 1988—Please, folks, this is not, repeat is *not* an encouragement to avoid condoms now. Flirting with pregnancy is one thing: having a kid can be a great celebration of life; flirting with AIDS is something else: is simply courting a quick and ugly death.

cobblestones. Came to a ferry landing, and embarked on a ferry for Jersey City, where we were followed and hooted at by a band of youngsters, bought bologna sandwiches at a local delicatessen, and found our way into the town cemetery, where we sat down on tombstones to eat and recite Keats to each other. A huge white dog came out of nowhere and laid his head on my lap like a unicorn in an old tapestry while I sat on the tombstone, and immediately the bleeding started. This is a method of abortion that I highly recommend, though I have never heard of anyone else who tried it, either successfully or unsuccessfully. Only thing was, when it was time to go back to Manhattan, we could find no ferry and were told by the bus driver who took us to the Hudson tube that the ferry hadn't run in several years. . . .

Later, after I moved uptown, I got a diaphragm at the Sanger Clinic, with much trepidation and lying about being married, and I would scramble out of bed in that freezing cold-water flat, and go into the room called the Woodshed, where I would stand, trembling with cold, as I slipped the small rubber disk into place. And by the time I came back, shivering and with cold feet, to the bed, it would be a matter of starting all over again, of somehow *working up to* the passion we had set so easily and naturally going in the first place.

Well, you may flatter yourself, that's all in the past, the lucky girls have the pill now, and they can do what they please, are as free as men, etc., etc. The pill, the pill, the pill! I am so tired of hearing about the pill, hearing the praises of the pill! Let me tell you about the pill. It makes you fat, the pill does. It makes you hungry. Gives you sore breasts, slight morning sickness, condemns you, who have avoided pregnancy, to live in a perpetual state of early pregnancy: woozy, and nauseous, and likely to burst into tears. And—crowning irony—it makes you, who have finally achieved the full freedom to fuck, much less likely to want to fuck, cuts down on the sex drive. So much for the pill.

Then there is the cunning little gadget known as the IUD—intrauterine device. A funny little plastic spring they stick in your womb. Why not? Principle on which it works (they think) is that it drives your womb frantic, trying to get rid of it, and everything inside of you happens that much more quickly: the monthly egg passes through your system in two or three hours, instead of as many days. Only a few little things wrong with the IUD: cramps, intermittent bleeding, a general state of tension. It also has a habit of wandering, and may turn up just about anywhere, or not turn up at all. There are two strings attached to the clever little contraption and sticking out of the neck of your womb, and you are supposed to check, by poking around in your vagina, whether or not the strings are still there. Nobody had told me what you do about it if they aren't. Also, since the IUD does allow nature a narrow margin of functioning, there are a few hours when you *can* get pregnant, and, if you're going to get pregnant, I guess you probably will, in those few hours. Nurse once told me of delivering a baby with a coil embedded in the afterbirth.

What then? What does that leave us? Leaves us ye olde-fashioned diaphragm, and we all know what a drag that is, and ye almost-as-olde creams and foams, which purportedly can be used *without* a diaphragm, and are good for exactly twenty minutes to a half hour after insertion, which means you have to work pretty fast, with one eye on the clock. They also *drip* and run and are unspeakably gooey, and add to the natural joyous gooey-ness of lust a certain chemical texture and taste, which could, I suppose, with determination, become an acquired taste, but is at least slightly unpleasant to the uninitiated. And up you get, if *he* gets his up again, and you insert into all the gooey mess inside you some more foam. Medieval, I'd say.

Or it leaves us having babies. Having babies has certain advantages, not to be gainsaid. One is that you don't have to do anything about it—when you want to fuck, you just fuck. Nothing gooey, nothing tension-making. If you get knocked up, the discomfort of early pregnancy tends to last only two or three months—whereas with the pill it lasts forever. Pregnancy always makes me want to fuck more, too, and I enjoy it more. And in those last months, the delights of ingenuity are added, and many new joys discovered. As for childbirth, having a baby is a matter of lying down and having it. After the first one, nothing could be easier if you forget the rules: forget doctors, hospitals, enemas, shaving of pubic hair, forget stoicism and "painless childbirth"—simply holler and push the damned thing out. Takes less time, trouble, and thought than any of the so-called "modern methods of birth control." And to support the creature? Get welfare, quit working, stay home, stay stoned, and fuck.

* * *

Being a woman to three men was an interesting trip. Big Bill had eyes for me, but I put him off for a while. I didn't know how Billy would feel about it if I made it with his dad, and I dug him too much to fuck things up.

We finally got together one weekend when Billy and Little John were off on a two-day hike. After supper Big Bill just sat down on the sofa beside me and began to undo my shirt. His deliberation and assurance came on like restraint, and the man-smell of his body—sweat and earth and tobacco—was tremendously exciting to me. Except for being raped by Serge Klebert I had never made it with an older man, and I was pleasantly surprised. Big Bill's body was lean and hard, the muscles well-defined, steel-like under the smooth, mobile skin. His prick, when I drew it from his work pants, was slimmer than Billy's but slightly longer. It had a kind, worldly-wise air about it, as if it had drawn wisdom from all the cunts it had entered. There was a competence and strength in his long fingers as he took hold of me, a skill and understanding in his lips on my breast that was reassuring and delightful. I was about to embark on a voyage with a seasoned sailor, one who knew the trip and every turn of the wind. He made me sense my youth and awkwardness, and see them as something precious, not easily come by.

We passed a beautiful night on the couch, fucking and dozing till dawn. And then, when it turned light, we stumbled off to our separate beds for a few hours of sleep.

The scene with Little John was something else. We were too much alike in our littleness, our high energy and our toughness to interest each other. Though we did try making out once or twice experimentally in the afternoon when Big Bill and Billy were off at work and John had not yet gotten a job on the road crew with them, it never went anywhere and we never thought much about it, one way or the other.

Evenings would find the four of us listening to the world on Big Bill's short-wave radio—the outside world that seemed so far away from our farmhouse, but would suddenly loom: close, treacherous and threatening as soon as we turned the knob. Or we would play chess, or read plays together. Big Bill really dug amateur theatricals and his idea of the way to spend a country evening was to do staged readings. He had a good voice and was really fine at it: Shakespeare or Brecht, found Cocteau too thin, boomed lines at us while insects crash-landed by the thousands on the screens, attracted by our late-burning lights.

Yes, it was good, being a chick to three men, and each of them on his own trip, each wanting a different thing, so that the world filled out, and interplay, like a triple-exposed photo, made infinite space. I have since found that it is usually a good thing to be the woman of many men at once, or to be one of many women on one man's scene, or to be one of many women in a household with many men, and the scene between all of you shifting and ambiguous. What is not good, what is claustrophobic and deadening, is the regular one-to-one relationship. OK for a weekend, or a month in the mountains, but not OK for a long-time thing, not OK once you have both told yourselves that this is to be the form of your lives. Then begin endless claims, and jugglings to avoid boredom, and the slow inexorable closing of God's infinite horizon, like the red-hot tightening walls in Poe's "The Pit and the Pendulum," walls that move in inexorably and choke the life out of your world.

In the Middle Ages there was the chastity belt—but that at least could be dealt with, with a hacksaw if nothing else. In our parents' day there was marriage, there sometimes still is, and that is ugly enough, but it is a legal form, and can be dealt with by more of the same, more papers. It is unpleasant, but it is only one form of the monster. The real horror, the nightmare in which most of us are spending our adult lives, is the deep-rooted insidious belief in the one-to-one world. The world of "this is my old man." Live with one man, and you begin to have a claim on him. Live with five, and you have the same claim, but it is spread out, ambiguous, undefined. What is unfilled by one will be filled by another easily, no one hung up guilty and inadequate, no one pushed to the wall by demands that he/she can't meet.

I remember reading in the books of that great woman explorer, Alexandra David-Neel that in Tibet both polygamy and polyandry were once practiced freely. Would love to know more about that social structure, how it worked, how they got it to work, who lived with whom. In the photos the women are beautiful, strong, free creatures, sufficient to themselves; I read that they owned land and businesses like their menfolk; and the men—well, the men and women together created one of the wildest magics this planet has ever witnessed.

We flourished on our Hudson River farm, functioned for each other. Big Bill took care of my head—his largesse and stability, his confidence made me feel safe and well, as I had never felt in my life, his gallantry made me feel beautiful. Billy was fleshmate and comrade, we were well-matched: I could hold my own with him hiking, or weeding, or fucking; my life-force matched his well. And Little John was brother and friend; I heard my paranoia echoing in his head, he found his secrets spelled out in my poems. Many a stalemate game of chess went down between us.

It was a different life from any that I had known before: the quiet of those long twilights, when we would pass the grass around and mumble warm laconic sentences at each other in the bare, dowdy living room with its worn-out sofa and dumpy chairs. Billy sometimes singing to us; Big Bill reminiscing, telling anecdotes of Woody Guthrie, or running down the wartime rackets in New York City, filling us in; Little John scribbling in notebooks, biting his nails in a corner. I got used to the slow, spaced rhythm of my days and for a while it seemed to me that I had never known any other pace than this timeless one, days colored green by the garden, and nights colored gold by the oil lamp. I lost myself in my new-found woman's role, the position defined and revealed by my sex: the baking and mending, the mothering and fucking, the girls' parts in the plays—and I was content.

But slowly, imperceptibly, the days began to shorten, the grass turned brown, and with the first crickets a restlessness stirred in me for the quick combat and hard living of the city, for the play and the strife and the inexhaustible human interchange that was New York to me then. I would catch myself listening for the traffic, or the background sound of "Bird" being played on a cheap phonograph in the next apartment, and I knew it was time for me to be on my way. So I took my leave of Billy for the time being—he would be back in New York in the fall—gave him back his baggy Levis and donned my office skirt and blouse. Big Bill drove me to a bus station, and within an hour I was back in New York.

Chapter 10—Summer

You never do get to go *back* to anything, but it really takes a long time to learn that . . .

When I stepped off the bus at 40th Street and Eighth Avenue, it was like arriving at a foreign port. The city, steaming and tropical, resounded with music: guitars, harmonicas, an occasional horn, radios blaring, children playing in the dark, women talking together on the sidewalks or stoops, or calling to each other from the windows. The night was pregnant with lust and violence, and the small, dark men stalked softly. It was a universe away from the world of home-fries and roadwork that I had left only an hour and a half earlier, and yet it was the same, exactly the same—crowded together and seen in the dark.

Downtown the streets were filled with youngsters who had made their way to the Village over the summer months. You could hear the drumming blocks from Washington Square, and when you stepped into the crowd around the fountain, you saw the young men barefoot and naked to the waist, and the young women, their skirts held high, stomping and dancing together in the heavy night.

I had no luggage and I had no pad. The apartment had been lost for non-payment of rent while I was away, and O'Reilley had moved my "stuff"—mostly books—to a West Tenth Street apartment where a little street-hustler-ballet-dancer named René Strauss lived. I joined the kids at the fountain, chanting and clapping, greeting friends and acquaintances, hearing the news. Finally, the crowd thinned, the musicians all went home, and I wandered over to René's and fell out.

I spent the next few days casing the scene. The city was really crowded; there were, simply, no pads to be had, and rather than hassle I took to sleeping in the park.

At that time no laws had been passed limiting a citizen's right of access to the public parks, no curfews were in effect. By two o'clock in the morning Washington Square was usually clear of its usual crowd: folksingers, faggots, and little girls from New Jersey on the make, and I would stretch out on the steps by the fountain and sleep peacefully until just after dawn, when a Park Department man with a big broom would come by and wake me. He swept my bed and went away again, and I and the half-dozen other people, all complete strangers, who shared these quarters, would exchange dazed greetings and go back to sleep till ten or so, when people started to arrive.

There was a regular crew of about eight of us who slept there, four to six of the eight being there on any given night, and we all got to know each other pretty well, as far as moods and habits and aura went, but we never spoke. Something about the intimacy of our shared space and the code of coolness in effect at that time would have made it unseemly for us to know each other by name, or have anything more to say to each other than the minimum morning greeting. It would have been intrusion, filling each other's turf and head with rattling chatter and conversation, and the inevitable unfolding of our emotional lives would have destroyed the space that the indifference of the city gave each and every one as her most precious gift.

At ten I would get up, stretch, look around me, and read for an hour or so till I was thoroughly awake. Then, stuffing all my accoutrements into the attaché case that served as my portable home and contained a raincoat, a toothbrush, notebooks, pens, and a change of underwear, I would pick it up and set off for the Chinese laundry on Waverly Place. I kept all my clothes there on separate tickets: one pair of slacks and one shirt on each ticket. I would take out a ticket's worth, and, carrying now attaché case and laundry package, I'd amble to Rienzi's, which opened at eleven, and order a breakfast, usually some kind of sweet and espresso coffee, though occasionally I'd splurge and treat myself to eggs and English muffins, or even some sausages or bacon. While the order was making, I'd find my way to the bathroom which was hidden away downstairs; down a rank, damp staircase with oozing walls, and along a corridor straight out of the *Count of Monte Cristo* to a tiny, cramped room, fortunately vaguely cleaned, where I would wash my face and feet and hands, brush my teeth, and change clothes, stuffing the dirty ones into a paper bag I carried in the attaché case for that purpose. Would then pull a brush through my hair and tie it up, and, feeling vaguely human, would grope my way up the stairs and to my breakfast.

Great pleasure it is to sit in an unhurried, uncrowded shop, drinking good, strong coffee and reading while your friends come in and out and the morning draws to a close and you write stray words in a notebook. I would linger as long as I could, usually a couple of hours, leaving finally to go to my afternoon's "work." The man to whom Duncan Sinclair had been selling his pictures, a real porn tycoon named Nelson Swan, had been busted, and that market was dead for the moment, but I had found it simpler and pleasanter, though much less lucrative, to work for some of the older painters on the scene—painters who were one or two generations older than the abstract expressionists, and still used models.

They were gentle, friendly folk who had come of age during the depression and were given to painting what in the thirties had been known as "Social Realism"—people with a sad, haunting sense that the world had changed since their "day," and a persistent kindly determination to discover of what the change consisted. Most of them were within walking distance of Washington Square, and I would walk up to the studio where I was expected, stopping along the way to drop off the bag with my yesterday's clothes at the Chinese laundry. I would perch on a high stool, or recline on a couch, in Moses Soyer's studio, while his wife rattled in and out chattering and Moses told me the gossip about his other models: who was going to have a baby, who was leaving for San Francisco, and almost one could believe oneself in that haunting and haunted world of nineteenth-century Paris, would catch the bold and flashy faces from *La Bohème* out of the corners of one's eyes. The money I got for two hours modeling was enough to buy me dinner and next morning's breakfast and to take another outfit out of the laundry, and, as I had no other needs, I thought myself quite rich.

After a while a certain number of luxuries attached themselves to this routine: I met Victor Romero, a young photographer with a job and an apartment, and he gave me a key to his place, which had a shower; and occasionally I would work two jobs in one day and take René or O'Reilley out to dinner; and I got a card at the New York Public Library, which varied my reading considerably.

Then one day I wandered into the Quixote Bookstore on MacDougal Street and Norman Verne, the proprietor, offered me a job: he and his wife Gypsy wanted to go canoeing on the Canadian lakes for a month, and would I like to manage the store? The store came with a kitchen in the back, complete with stove and refrigerator, and there was an army cot to set up in the middle of the back room, where one could sleep in comparative luxury. The rains and thunderstorms of late August had begun, and the park was neither as pleasant nor as convenient as it had been, so I accepted, gave a few days' notice to all my painters, and moved in, attaché case and all, and Norm and Gypsy took off.

After they were gone, I discovered that the store also came with its own built-in junkie: a very beautiful, ghost-like blonde boy named Luke Taylor, who played a very

117

heavy shade blues guitar and shot a lot of heroin—"horse" as we called it then. I had seen Luke around the scene for some time—he used to frequent the Saturday night "rent parties" that were held in a loft around Twentieth Street and Seventh Avenue—and I had eyes for him from the first time I heard him sing. Something about the supercool, wasted look: the flattened, broken nose, the drooping green eyes, thin pinched junkie face with its drawn mouth—the mixture of hungry and bitter—cut right through me, and left me wanting to touch, to fondle, to somehow warm that chilly flesh. I was in love with Luke then, and for some time to come.

On the first night that I was talking care of the store— it opened around four in the afternoon and stayed open till midnight in order to cover the tourist trade—I was standing in the doorway, looking out at the scene on MacDougal Street. The Village had gotten tougher as the summer had worn on. It was one of those years in the middle of the nineteen-fifties when the Italians who lived below Bleecker Street, getting more and more uptight behind the huge influx of "new Bohemians" (the word "beatnik" had not yet been coined) were beginning to retaliate with raids and forays into what we had traditionally considered our territory: the streets north of Bleecker. On their side, it must be admitted that we were invading, moving into their turf *en masse*. Many new apartments on Sullivan Street, Thompson Street, etc., had been opened up to us by the real estate moguls. They were cheap, convenient to the Village scene, and in the heart of the Italian neighborhood. Into them flocked unheeding the boys and girls of the new

Village: men who wore sandals, or went barefoot, and sometimes wore jewelry, girls who favored heavy eye make-up and lived with a variety of men, outright faggots, and—worst crime of all to the Italian slum mind—racially mixed couples.

The police were run by Tammany Hall, and Tammany was itself the heart of the Italian Village, and so they tended to ignore the escapades of the Italian youth. Only two days before, I had stood in Washington Square and watched a police car cruise slowly up the block and away, while about twenty young men pursued François, a quiet, pale-skinned mulatto boy from the Bahamas, into a building then under construction. The twenty hoodlums milled about in the empty lot next door, shouting obscenities and afraid to enter the building, till someone started, and they all took up, the chant "Get a pipe! Get a pipe!" The police car pulled smoothly away to the tune of this bloodthirsty chant, with never a backward glance. François, whom I knew slightly, had been making it with Linda, a pretty white chick of about sixteen, since he hit the Village at the beginning of the summer.

On this particular evening, I stood on the steps of my new store and watched three young faggots get beaten up by their dago brothers. A not unusual evening's entertainment. A cool breeze was coming up and many people were out enjoying the soft summer air. The young men ducked into a hallway two doors away from me. Scuffling and screams. The police pulled up. They bravely entered the building, arrested the three gay men and drove away. About three minutes later, the young gangsters emerged from the building and continued their stroll up the block.

Somebody came into the shop and asked for *Vestal Lady on Brattle*, Gregory Corso's first book, which had just been printed in Cambridge. There was no "beat poetry" as yet, it was just another poetry book. After the customer left, I settled down on the stoop to read a copy. I was deep into Gregory's peculiarly beautiful head when Luke appeared, guitar in hand.

"Where's Norm?" he asked hoarsely. His voice was always hoarse, was hardly more than a whisper, with that peculiar junk roughness.

"He's gone," I said, "for four weeks. Gone camping with Gypsy in Canada."

Luke muttered some obscenity, started to take off, then came back and sat down beside me on the metal steps.

"You watching the store?" he asked.

I nodded.

"You gonna be sleeping here?" he persisted, edging toward the thing that was on his mind.

I nodded again. Supercool, me too.

"Oh," he said. He was silent for a few minutes, and we both watched the street.

Then he said, "I was living in back here. Didn't Norm tell you?"

Now, Norm had told me nothing—whether because he wanted to cool the scene with Luke and was hoping I would get rid of him, or for whatever reasons of his own, I didn't know.

"No," I said. I was quite surprised. One of the things I had really been looking forward to was having that combi-

120

nation kitchen-bedroom all to myself, and cooking little things, and puttering, and playing the hi-fi: playing house, for all the world as if it were mine, and mine alone. After you've been on the streets for a while, living alone becomes the ultimate luxury.

I was quiet, but Luke, I was sure, could hear me thinking, with that telepathy people develop when they are continually at the mercy of others. I glanced sidelong at him and my heart went out to him. I wanted to touch those long, skinny, dirty fingers—beautifully articulate hands with the mercilessly bitten nails. A pang of desire shot like lightning through my groin.

"No, I didn't know you were staying here," I said softly, "but if you want to, I guess you still can. I mean—we can figure something out so we both fit." I didn't look at him. "Why don't you go on back and stash your guitar?"

"Yeah," he said, and I met his eyes, and he flashed a smile. "Yeah, thanks. All I want to do right now is fall out."

I went back with him, and helped him set up the cot, and he flung himself across it, declining blankets and food, and in a moment was deeply asleep.

The street got dark, a few people came and bought books. I read the rest of *Vestal Lady on Brattle*, but all the while my head was in the back room with Luke, anticipating the night. I felt as if someone had laid a rare gift in my hands.

At last it was midnight and I locked the front door and turned out the lights in the front of the store. I poked my head in back and Luke was still sound asleep, so I decided to go out for a while and ramble. The street was extraordinarily quiet and, after checking out the scene at Rienzi's and the Limelight, I realized that I hadn't eaten supper and was very hungry, and that Luke would probably be hungry too when he woke up. There was a deli on Seventh Avenue that was open all night, and there I bought frozen potato pancakes and jars of apple sauce and cokes for a late meal.

When I got back to the store on MacDougal Street it was about three in the morning. I let myself in and groped my way to the narrow back room without turning any lights on. I found the refrigerator and stuck the bag of groceries in without unpacking it. The light from inside fell across Luke's face, and he stirred and half-opened his eyes. He had been up for a while, I figured, because the amplifier of the hi-fi set was glowing orange in the dark. I switched it off, and slipped out of my clothes, terribly aware of Luke, awake and silent in the dark.

I found a blanket, wrapped myself in it, and lay down beside him on the cot, feeling him move over slightly to make room for me, feeling his hard, tense body next to mine in the dark, his clothes and my blanket between us. He reached out and traced my face and neck in the dark, ending with a brotherly squeeze of my shoulder.

"You OK?" he mumbled. "You got enough room? 'Cause I can sleep on the floor."

"No," I said, "I'm fine. You?"

"OK," he whispered. "I'm just OK, I guess." I could sense his smile in the dark.

I must have dozed off, because when I opened my eyes again it was light with the grey light of pre-dawn and Luke, stretched on his side, leaning on his elbow, his chin in his hand, looked down on me.

He smiled when I opened my eyes.

"Can't you sleep?" I asked him.

"Slept enough, I guess," and he bent down, and I reached up, and we found ourselves kissing.

My shyness with Luke—the shyness that always comes over me when I really have eyes for someone—had disappeared while I slept. Our kiss went on and on, and it seemed to me that the darkness had returned, and my hands fumbled in the dark to remove the clothes that hid that lean, tense body from me. He was wearing a red and black flannel work shirt, and I unbuttoned it blindly and slipped it off him licking and kissing at his chest. But when I started on the zipper of his fly, he caught my hands and held them still.

"Hey," he said gently, "hey." He unwound the blanket that was wrapped around me, brushed the hair out of my eyes, and began to nuzzle my breasts and stroke my sides.

I looked down at the thin dirty fingers on my shoulder, and they were trembling. I covered them with my own and drew them down to my breast, holding them with a warm steady pressure till the trembling stopped, and then drawing his hand on down to my cunt. His fingers closed over it, pressing clit and opening, but did not enter, and I was left in the grip of a warm, sickly feeling of desire alleviated but not satisfied. I slid my hands around his shoulders and drew him down to me, kissing him again and again on that thin, hungry mouth, drinking the bitterness and hurt, the sickly taste of endless lonely junksick mornings, the anger and coldness that translated as containment, or shyness.

His hand tightened over my cunt and the other slipped around and under my waist and held me close. I kissed his eyelids, the skin under his closed eyes, the bridge of his nose. Suckled at his eyebrows, smoothing his temples and the hollows of his gaunt cheeks with my lips. My hands slipped down inside his jeans, and he let go of me long enough to slip out of them, so that my palms curved concave against the hollows in his lean buttocks. My right hand slid down, one finger sunk deep into his asshole, the others stroking the skin behind his balls. I could feel his cock grow still larger against the soft flesh of my stomach. My cunt convulsed in a spasm that left me moist and aching with desire.

Luke's hand stirred against me, and he thrust two fingers deep into my wet cunt with long, sure strokes, moving slow and heavy as the blues he played. A moan escaped me, and I began to move in the preliminary rhythms of orgasm, but I wanted to prolong this moment, to suck the juice and essence, the very marrow and soul of this man I had wanted for so long. And so I shifted slightly, almost imperceptibly, my mounting excitement lost a bit of its edge, the mists cleared momentarily.

My finger in his asshole began to rotate slowly, moving in larger and larger circles, and the fingers that were stroking him found his balls and caressed them with a touch infinitely light and tender. I slid my free hand between my stomach and his, and closed my fingers over his cock. I felt as if I were fainting.

A feeling of utter surrender swept over me, I knew I belonged to him totally, to his hunger and darkness and magic. I wanted him to mark me permanently with some mark that proclaimed me his, to enter all of my orifices at once, to leave me utterly used, spent, exhausted as I had never been, while I felt peace grow in him at last, and I became the ground devoured to feed and suckle the small, deeply buried seed of his joyousness. All of my flesh seemed to melt, to grow into his, as my hand moved up and down on his huge, stiff cock, and he, divining something of my thoughts, set his teeth against my shoulder and drew blood, with a pain that was ecstasy itself.

Then he moved above me, I threw my two legs over his shoulders as his hands on my shoulders drew me against him, and I could feel the walls of my cunt stretch taut to contain the huge cock which filled me to the bursting. I could hardly bear it, and my cries of pain and ecstasy filled the small, littered room, my head rolled from side to side on the small cot, and my hands on his buttocks drew him to me again and again as he lunged with fierce, searing strokes that seemed to penetrate the very core of my being. When I came, in a great, bursting flood of light, I felt as if I must literally die, that my flesh could not possible contain the current that was flowing through it, and I heard a voice that I realized must be my own filling the room with short, stabbing animal cries as I slipped into darkness.

The roar of the waves slowly receded, leaving me high and dry on a white beach, in a blinding white light. I opened my eyes and met Luke's slanting green ones, glazed and distant. I watched for a long time while the glint of human consciousness slowly returned to them. His lips moved dimly. "God," he said hoarsely, in his indistinct undertone. "God, I think I love you."

"Hush," I said, "hush," pulling his head against my breast. For to name it was to make it less than it was.

We lay together for a long time without moving again. In vain did the sunshine pour into the sordid little room, insisting that it was day, that this was the dusty, cluttered back room of a Village bookstore, that we were, in fact, two rather young, rather vulnerable human creatures on an uncomfortable army cot. We two were one seed form, one kernel, nested in darkness, in hard shell, dark and smooth inside, whose downy exterior cushioned us from sound and motion. We two, one seed form, nestled close and together in our own germinating warmth till the long fingers of light and wind should find us and coax us back into being.

"Pre-matter energy," I thought dreamily, thinking of Reich, and realized I had been touched at last, had been truly entered, that there was a dark core of mystery in our coming together that I would never penetrate.

We lay there together as long as we could, at first oblivious to everything but each other, and then later trying not to be moved by the noises of the traffic, the bustle of the outside, the increasingly warm sun that was pouring in through the back window of the shop. We were hungry and we had to go to the bathroom, but every time one of us moved an experimental limb the other would clasp him (or her) tighter and nestle closer.

Finally hunger won the day, and with one quick movement I slid out of Luke's arms, stood up, and made for the refrigerator with its stash of goodies. I put up a pot of coffee, and was just opening the package of frozen potato pancakes, cutting into the brightly colored plastic wrapper with the point of a paring knife, when Luke came up behind me and put his arms around my waist, and I could feel his hard, full cock jabbing at my buttocks. He said nothing, just pulled me close and hard up against him with those lean tense arms of his, and tried to get his cock in between the two mounds of my ass, into my asshole.

I went limp at his touch, melted up against him, fitting my body to his, and when I sensed what he wanted I bent at the waist, leaning over the table to help him get in. But I was too tight, and he drew me away from the table, and the next thing I knew I was lying face down on the floor, spread-eagled with Luke straddling me. He must have reached the cooking oil down from the table, for his hands, covered with oil, were all over my ass and into my asshole. As his lean, powerful fingers entered my anus, I cried out, I nearly fainted with a pleasure that was at the same time an unappeasable longing, an aching desire that I felt somehow could never be satisfied. Then his hands tugged at me, raising my haunches as his big, full cock entered me. He lay full length on me, his hand on my cunt, pressing into the hard, gritty floor, his thin mouth sucking and nipping at my shoulders.

When I first hit the ground I had put my hands under my head to cushion my face, protect it from the dirty floorboards, but my desire to touch him, to caress him any way I could, was too much for me, and, even as I was pounded, ground into the worn linoleum by the rapidly increasing rhythms of his lust, my hands came around and stroked and caressed his sides, his buttocks, and my feet came up to stroke his thin, muscular legs.

There was a blindness to his passion that set up a momentary resistance in me. I was being used as I had never been used, and I was not sure that I liked it, could rise to meet this demand; but the tremulous insistence of his hand in my cunt—through the wall of which, I knew, he could feel his cock pulsing and lunging in my ass—and the blind force of his passion, breaking through his flesh and tangling with his mouth in my hair, cut through all thought, and I heard myself crying out that he should never stop, and then crying again and again in a wordless rage of pain and pleasure that was a hymn of praise to the light of ecstasy exploding in us both.

I got off the floor, dirty, disheveled and bruised, and with oil on my ass, and went on with the business of preparing breakfast. Or whatever meal it was. The sun, it seemed, was going down. The store hadn't been opened. Some semblance of responsibility led me now to throw a trench coat around myself and tape a scribbled note to the front door: "Sorry, Closed Today. Will Open Tomorrow As Usual." I puttered a while, straightening up the store, and went back again to the back room in the dusk now, and found Luke nodding out at the table, a towel around his waist, having turned on in the hall john, and my heart sank a little, but I said nothing; instead I put the "Carmina Burana" on the hi-fi, but soft, and sat down with Hesse's *Demian* to read a little. In those days Hesse had not been reprinted, was in English only in an early, out-of-print edition, and was eagerly seized upon whenever it turned up. It got dark. I switched on a lamp, brewed a pot of coffee, and switched from Carl Orff to the Modern Jazz Quartet, "Django."

After a while Luke stirred, and I gave him some coffee without saying anything, not knowing where he was at, or if he wanted to talk, and he drank it, watching me over the cup while I sat reading, or pretending to read, till I heard his gruff, half-pleading "Come here," and went to him immediately, kneeling by his chair, my head in his lap, while he stroked my hair, wordless, and I finally turned my head and untied his silly little towel and found his cock with my lips. And slowly, slowly, under the long, gentle ministrations of my mouth and tongue it grew hard, and in the slow, hot, summer night with all the noises of August backyards and August streets exploding around us, I made love to that thick, strong, uncircumcised cock, made love indeed, called love into being, coaxed it into fullness and feeling with my mouth—I was young enough and had magic enough to do that. In love, I MADE love, and love flowered like a aureole around us both, and my mouth moved slowly, endlessly, tirelessly, slipping and plunging on that thick, full member, till it began to buck and press against my palate like some wild and eager bird seeking freedom, and I moved faster and faster, and a great sigh that was the lifebreath itself escaped from Luke, and I drank in his seed, drank in his bitter, crystal seed in great eager gulps, as if to bring us together finally and for all time, so that no change, nothing and no one, could put us apart again. My hands were on his fine, thin waist as he came, I could feel his back arch, the electricity in his flesh, and my head between his strong, golden-haired thighs was clasped tightly, I could hear his blood—or my own—exploding in my ears, and knew this seed I swallowed for the sacrament—the holy and illimitable essence that drove the stars.

Then he bent and kissed my mouth to taste himself, and we sat for a long time in the summer night, my hair tumbled over his lap, his hands cupping my shoulders. When at last we groped our way back to our cot and slept, it was the wondering and joyous sleep of children on Christmas Eve; we kept waking up and touching each other, simply to taste the magic.

Chapter 11—The Pad:One

Luke and I didn't get much time together. It was only a couple of weeks after our first scene that he came back to the store one night looking white as a sheet, and told me he was going to have to split town for a while. He said he had been walking on Thompson Street—it was about three o'clock in the morning—and had seen two people sticking a third one, unconscious, under the wheels of a truck while somebody else started up the engine. He said he had just kept going, and didn't think they had seen him, but the guy under the truck was someone he knew by sight; somebody who had been dealing pot in Mafia territory. At that point, mid-nineteen-fifties New York, all the dealing was heavily controlled and apportioned block by block. You didn't sell anything—not even single joints—outside your appointed territory. Luke had been doing some freelance dealing himself, and he figured to get out while the getting was good.

"Where are you going?"

"I dunno. Maybe New Orleans."

New Orleans was still a possible town in those days, a

good place to stay stoned, lie low—make it somehow. It has since dropped off the map except for purposes of professional revolution—anyway, I haven't heard of anyone except SNCC or SDS making it to New Orleans in years. But at that time it was a pretty hip town, full of dope and alcohol and easy living.

The first of the pre-beat "little magazines" written in the "hip" argot we all devotedly and self-consciously spoke, had just come out of New Orleans. It was called *Climax* and was edited, typed, printed, and stapled by a handsome blonde adventurer named Bob Cass. *Climax* combined literature and jazz news. Jazz was for us the most important, happening art; the first spokesmen in our idiom spoke trumpet and sax: Bird in Louis' Tavern on West Fourth Street on weekday nights handed out posters for his incredible weekends at the Open Door on West Broadway, weekends when he would take us all with him, teach us all to fly. And later, Miles at the Cafe Bohemia, slick and smart as they come, exchanging sets with Charlie Mingus, cool then and cool now, but no electricity in him, didn't break barriers, or we didn't hear it then—though he changed in the sixties, or I did—and we would wander outside while Mingus played, get some air, and duck back in to hear Miles' driving horn bringing it home again and again.

Later the jazz men were followed by the painters, a big, hulking breed of hard-drinking men who spoke in oils and came on very paternal and sexy. They got their hands on a lot of loot and threw it around, and set a certain style for the late fifties, more moneyed and faster-moving. Proud.

But that was later. Just then Luke said "New Orleans"

and I really heard him. Saw the wrought-iron balconies and the haze of heat and dust. Saw the slow-moving smiling people getting high in the sun, drinking black coffee down in the French market, the big boats unloading fruit and fish, large healthy gulls screaming and turning, and nearly said "I'm going with you." We both could hear the words hanging silent in the dusty room, the room waited, but I didn't speak.

Two things held me back. One was our code, our eternal tiresome rule of Cool, that would have made it impossible for me to say those words without blowing our entire scene, retrospectively even, blowing what had gone before, so that if I had indeed gone with Luke all the magic would have gone out of our coming together—or so it seemed to us then. The other was my total, unutterable fascination with Manhattan, a love affair with the city that I was in the midst of, caught up in, it turned out, for many years. An overwhelming love of the alleys and warehouses, of the strange cemetery downtown at Trinity Church, of Wall Street in the dead of night, Cathedral Parkway on Sunday afternoons, of the Chrysler building gleaming like fabled towers in the October sun, the incredible prana and energy in the air, stirring a creativity that seemed to spring from the fiery core of the planet and burst like a thousand boiling volcanoes in the music and painting, the dancing and the poetry of this magic city. So, instead of speaking, I took his hand.

"When are you going?" I asked him.

"This morning," he said. "I thought I'd get on the road when it got light."

He went to the back room and began stuffing his few things into a beat-up old rucksack. I followed after him and turned on the hi-fi. Vivaldi's "Gloria Mass." I put some lamb chops in the broiler and started cutting up lettuce with a vengeance. He might as well eat, I figured, before he split.

Then Luke came over and touched the back of my hand, and I looked up at him and he saw that there were tears in my eyes.

"Hey," he said softly to me. "Hey, girl."

His arms were around me, and I was clinging to his mouth as if I would never stop, and his hands were loosening my hair, and we were somehow naked and lying wrapped desperately close on the floor mattress that had replaced the army cot. He drew my two legs over his shoulders, pausing to kiss them from ankle to ass, biting with short sharp bites on the cheeks of my ass, and I felt his cock in my cunt, like coming home, like the most natural and only complete state of being, and felt it leave and, covered with my juice, enter my asshole, tearing in, not carefully now, but with a kind of desperation, while he sucked and bit at my arms and breasts. I was crying now, and I thought to go completely mad, for my longing was for some fulfillment more than the human body has devised, and at last his mouth closed over mine, and he lay full length on top of me, his cock in my wet, pulsing cunt, and we moved together grinding and pumping, moved together through time and eternity, and out, beyond space, where galaxies exploded and began, and watched the worlds as they slowly, harmoniously began to move again. When we came to I was lying on his chest, kissing his eyelids again and again, drinking his silent tears while my own dropped unheeded.

It was light. The lamb chops were hopelessly burned, the room full of smoke. I ran about, opening windows and cursing, while Luke got himself together. Then we both got into our clothes and went out to an all-night place on Sixth Avenue, the old Waldorf Cafeteria where we had occasionally gone together to watch Max Bodenheim cavort, and ate lamb stew and pickles and rolls and drank coffee after coffee, and at last Luke picked up his pack and slung it on, and I walked him to the bus which would take him to a favored hitchhiking spot near the Lincoln Tunnel, and waited till he got on. We said goodbye without touching, our eyes barely meeting in the dusty August wind.

And then, within two weeks Norm and Gypsy came back from their camping trip and the warm comfort of the bookstore was gone. It was too hectic by now to be on the streets and the dawns were chilly sometimes, so I took the money I had saved and rented a pad that Dirty John was leaving: a cold-water flat uptown on 60th Street, where Tenth Avenue becomes Amsterdam Avenue, at the north end of Hell's Kitchen. It was a good big pad with high ceilings and a fireplace in the large front room, two middle rooms of fair size, and a real hole of a kitchen with the bathtub next to the sink—the tub had a cover you used to drain the dishes—an antique stove decorated in green enamel with a high oven and three burners, and a small greasy window looking out on an airshaft. It was a good pad because of the size of the front room, because the fireplace worked, and because it cost thirty-three dollars a month.

The john was in the hall, was unspeakably dirty, and could not be cleaned no matter what, because it was only one flight up and therefore used by every bum in the neighborhood who was sober enough to make it up the stairs. On cold mornings we would often find a body or two asleep there. Impossible to lock, the only thing that ever happened when we tried to lock it was the lock got stolen, ripped out of the rotten wood. Impossible to keep toilet paper, or even light bulbs, in there: such was the poverty of the place that both were copped immediately. When you went to the john you took toilet paper and light bulb in with you. Or if no spare bulb was handy, you took the flashlight which was kept on top of the refrigerator.

It was a lovely pad, one of the best I ever had, and I look back on it with great fondness to this day. The life I lived in it was the simplest, kindest, and most devoted life I have ever managed to live, the friends were fine, the goals were clear and set.

When we first moved in there was just me and Susan O'Reilley. We made a real living room of the front room, with an old studio couch that had been left behind by a former tenant, roommate of Dirty John's; an ancient drawing table; a desk and chair from my parents' house; and a few long benches of weathered, unpainted wood which we had stolen off the construction lots of newly-fashionable high-rise apartment buildings. The benches we were especially fond of, because when we ran out of firewood we burned them without compunction and simply went out for more as they were needed.

We slept in the larger of the two middle rooms, on a bed

that was nothing but a bed frame with some wooden slats across it and an old cotton-stuffed mattress on top of that. The lumpiest and most uncomfortable bed I ever slept in, ten times more uncomfortable than sleeping on the floor, but we were somehow attached to the idea of Bed, of being raised off the floor. The bedroom had a door to the outside, which we bolted with a two-by-four and huge iron bolts after Little John, who is not to be confused with Dirty John, and who was by then O'Reilley's ex-lover, broke in and took the place apart while looking for her (she and I having hitchhiked to Cambridge to get out of his way). Over the bolted door we hung a precarious bookcase. And that, and an ancient desk, relic of my childhood which we carted out of Brooklyn in a borrowed van, completed the furnishings of the "bedroom."

The smaller middle room we immediately dubbed The Woodshed and filled with cartons and barrels of wood for the fireplace: wood copped off construction sites, or donated by the place around the corner between Tenth Avenue and the river which crated automobiles for shipping overseas. No one in those days had heard of beatniks or hippies, and so the guys who worked there were cheerful and friendly, and cut us lots of good red oak whenever their boss was away, cut it to the size of our fireplace on their powerful electric saws, grinning and talking the while as we stood in the bright, chilly place with our shopping carts, the acrid smell of the cut wood and the clear chilly air off the river making us high. It took about four cartloads a day to keep us warm, but on good days when the scrap barrels were full, or when we felt particularly energetic, we would get many more and fill the woodshed even fuller for the colder times to come. Woodshed was a word we were very fond of, because of Mezz Mezzrow's book, *Really the Blues*, which was one of the things we read that filled our heads with a way of talking and a way of being, and in it the word "woodshedding" is what you do when you hole up and practice your art, in his case jazz, to the exclusion of all else. Woodshedding was pretty much the rule of life at the Amsterdam Avenue pad, and a Woodshed made it even more so, more real. The only thing in the room besides the endless boxes of wood and a long low pile of two-by-fours and four-by-fours to saw up in a real emergency, was an old, unfinished dresser full of all our clothes and on top of it a file drawer full of all our collected works.

That was about it. When Susan and I arrived the house was awash in slivers of wood and tiny bits of paper, chewed and clawed by rats into all kids of comfy and luxurious rat-dwellings. It took us a full month to get the garbage out, and for months there was a large charred hole in the floor, right in front of the fireplace. "Oh that," said Dirty John, when he showed us the place, "was where I dropped a burning log and forgot to pick it up." The beams under the floor were charred and partly gone: the house must have come close to burning down. One day the following spring a good dyke friend arrived with electric saw and spent two or three days carefully fitting pieces of firewood into the hole and making the floor good and whole again, but for that first winter we lived with it as it was, and a wind came through it.

Soon after we moved in, René Strauss, our street hustler

friend from downtown, came to stay with us and the couch in the living room became a bed. René was a good roommate: almost never home, he turned up whenever he scored some money and took us gleefully out to breakfast. His scathing remarks on our lives and affairs—in the mordant tradition of "faggot wit"—kept us in humor and perspective most of the time. His two flaws were that he stole all our best clean clothes to wear when he went out cruising, and always refused to get out of bed in the morning.

Getting out of bed in the morning wasn't easy, as it was cold and got colder as time went on. I would usually do it first, and stomp about putting on Levis and sweatshirt (my eternal costume), and brushing my crew-cut (I had by then cut my hair). Then I'd pull on my stolen, black leather, fur-lined gloves, slide into a motorcycle jacket given me by Little John (we were the same size), pull on my black army-surplus boots, and, armed with the shopping cart, go out for wood. Two or three trips up the stairs with a full cart did wonders towards waking me up and getting my circulation going, and I would start a fire and make an enormous pot of oatmeal, singing and muttering the while, in order to warn René, who had probably come in at dawn, and O'Reilley, who could always sleep longer, no matter how long she had slept, that I was about to wake them. Coffee made and oatmeal bubbling, I would stand in the front room and loudly and obnoxiously announce breakfast to the snoring, blanket-clutching household, and the day would begin.

Chapter 12—The Pad: Two

Winter came. René moved out, went off to live with a sad but wealthy man on Central Park West who would pay for his ballet classes. The house became a ship braving an incredible storm; smokestacks on Eleventh Avenue stood out in the clear air like some kind of masts, landmarks or beacons. The science of survival became the science of fire-making. We were five now, a tight little family with a life-style, a form and jargon of our own.

There was Pete, who went to the Art Students' League in the mornings and painted in the afternoons in our large, sunny front room. He had started off as a child actor on Broadway, gone to Professional Children's School as a teenager, and finally dropped out of the acting game to become a painter. Pete was quiet; slow, dumpy and whimsical. He drew unicorns for hours, or strange, three-legged beasties with sad eyes, or filled huge pieces of masonite with calico landscapes over which wandered childlike phosphorescent creatures shaped like geodesic domes with antennae. He drew on paper, on the floor, on the walls, on napkins, sheets, and dirty windowpanes. He was good and happy.

There was Don. Don was long and thin, mulatto and gorgeous, an actor in the then still-current Actors' Studio tradition. Withdrawn, with large broody black eyes, thin nervous hands that played drums on anything, with anything, to the jazz in his head. Surprisingly gentle, whenever he did look out at you from the mist of dreams and sounds he lived behind, as if behind a glittering beaded curtain.

Don was O'Reilley's lover. She had had a really bad time with Little John over the summer: madness and abortions, and through it all John spouting half-digested Reichian psychology at her, and she wanted something cool and quiet. She got it. It was perhaps Don's excessive beauty that drove him into himself. Everyone wanted him. When the winter got out of hand, poverty too much for us to handle, it was Don who would go visit one or another of the Broadway people in the strange and unknown land of the East Sixties and come back with steaks and vodka and money. We heard through the grapevine that Montgomery Clift among others had a crush on him, and that it was he who was supplying these goodies, but Don wouldn't talk about it, would merely hand me meat or cash, turn on a record, and go sit down by the fire.

Then there was Leslie. Leslie was our faggot. Every house needs one, to keep it cheered up and silly, to take care of the plants and the candles, to bring some style into slum living. Leslie had been a pianist, but while studying at the Julliard School of Music had been compelled by the requirements of the curriculum to take a modern dance

142

class. This class completely amazed him and turned him on. He began to discover his body, to go downtown for ballet class, and he eventually threw over ten years of concert piano prep and dropped out of Julliard—he was on scholarship—to go to the Ballet Theatre School and become a dancer. He was beautiful and sad and fragile and gay. And gaily, wistfully, in love with Susan.

Both Ballet Theatre and the Art Students' League were within three or four blocks of the house, and our lives centered on the West Fifties all that year, becoming more closed and tight as we all settled down to our first year of serious work. In the morning Leslie and Pete would leave for their respective classes, Don would put on a record—a scratchy Miles rendition of "Walking" or some early Billie Holiday, on our twelve-dollar phonograph ("box" as we then called it). O'Reilley would stretch out on the couch in front of the fire and immerse herself in Spengler's *Decline of the West*, all two of which fat and morose volumes she read in the course of that winter, taking notes the while. I would study Homeric Greek out of an 1890s grammar I had discovered in my aunt's attic in Queens. At lunchtime we would all go out, to gather either at the cafeteria of the Art Students' League, or at the Chock Full O'Nuts across from Ballet Theatre. There we would eat such twenty-five-cent sandwiches as we could afford: lettuce and tomato, or cream cheese on date-nut bread, and exchange the news and discoveries of the morning over cups of extra-sweet coffee.

The afternoon would find us all at work again: me and Susan scribbling in notebooks, Pete drawing elaborate still lifes of the coffeepot or the chair, and Leslie off to another class or a rehearsal. Don would go down to Cromwell's Drugstore, the hangout for out-of-work actors who were supposedly making the rounds, where he would consume his fifty-cent minimum and listen to his friends talk shop. If the day was fine, Pete and Susan and I would take our notebooks to Central Park and scramble among the rocks or watch the ducks between poems and drawings; if not, we would stay home and huddle around the fire, or type on our ancient and decrepit typewriter with fingers stiff with cold.

The southern boundary of our world was Fiftieth Street, where there was a Longley's Cafeteria in which all of the coffee after the first cup was free, and poisonous—it being left all afternoon on hotplates with the cream already in it growing thick and curdly. There we would sometimes hide ourselves to read or write the afternoon away, watching the folk enter and leave, and making the acquaintance of some of the loquacious and eccentric old people for whom New York then still had time and space.

Within these limits were to be found the Donnell Library which had just opened, with its clean, glorious bathrooms, plenteous hot water and warmth, rugs in the sitting area, comfortable couches, and records to take out; and the Museum of Modern Art, to which we had year-long three-dollar artists' passes, which let us in free to see an endless stream of Dietrich, von Stroheim, Lang, Garbo, etc., turning us on for the first time to what that world of celluloid and flickering darkness was really about.

The Museum also boasted a cafeteria with seats on an inner courtyard, where we could sit among pretentious sculpture when the weather was fine, and drink and eat a fifty-cent afternoon tea consisting of tiny tasteless sandwiches and pale burnt-sienna liquid; and a penthouse restaurant, to which our three-dollar passes did not admit us. However, we had found a way up a back staircase that let us slip unnoticed into the penthouse, and would often repair thither to meet some of Pete's or Don's more prosperous actor friends who affected the more costly yearly memberships and bought us slender pastries while we listened to the theatre gossip.

And the paintings. In those days one could still manage to see the paintings at the Museum of Modern Art—it's been years since I've been able to do so. Nowadays there are always Heads, millions of Heads, between me and any work of art. If it's an opening night, the heads are likely to be well-groomed and finely perfumed. If not, they are apt to affect the latest Ohio hairstyles and Sears Roebuck coats, and to be equipped with loud, raucous voices. But in any case, there is no hope of seeing a painting unless you steal it, and take it home, and lock the door, hang it on your wall, and sit down. But then there weren't really very many people at museums, especially during the week, and one could settle quietly in the Brancusi room (holy, dusty air like a church) or on a hard bench in front of the Monet "Waterlilies" (since burned up), and scribble and daydream and feast on detail and color, or walk around a sculpture, examining it from all angles, backwards, or lying down under it, and scribble, and pick your teeth, and write a letter, and scribble, and take off your shoes. . . .

The northern limit of our country was Sixty-Fifth Street. It was there that Raphael Soyer had his studio in a musty old building known as the Lincoln Arcade, with spaced-out wrought-iron elevator cages and spaced-out elevator operators, and many teeming pimps and dealers and hustlers and housewives bustling about the ground floor where the shops were, and the lovely off-white light and opulent solidity of the areas of New York that were built during the last days of American prosperity, during the end of the nineteenth century. That area is now Lincoln Center, where I went once and thought I was in an airline terminal, and tried to see a movie, and it was like seeing a movie in a hospital, or a refrigerator. But then there were still Czechoslovakian voice teachers, Russians who had studied with Jung, violinists from the Balkans, Latvian translators, little professional people in big coats, living in that area, bundled and brisk at the markets, and I would go there about three days a week and sit in the airy, still light of Raphael's studio and he would paint me and ask me sad patient questions about my house and life, wondering at it all sadly, but constantly curious, like a rather bold sparrow. Or Susan and I would go together. He did a huge painting of the two of us naked and standing together, holding hands in front of a rumpled bed, a painting that he then considered too outrageous to show, and after working on it for three or four months, put it away for as many years.

On West Sixty-Fifth Street, too, was my modest equivalent of Don's outrageous luxury: a shrill-voiced, angular, sad-eyed psychology major named Betty McPeters, who had a crush on me and fed us all steaks and strawberries in her tiny West Side apartment every week or so in order to get me to come over for the evening. Betty's desires never managed to get even vaguely sexual; the most she could do was to stroke my hair, or my hand, purring "nice," like a cat. A pathetic creature. We would sit on her couch or her rug and devour huge amounts of food and chat with her friends: a Lower East Side book-thief-turned-priest named Bradley Dumpkin and a round, jolly black earth mother, Beatrice Harmon, who at last count had had four babies and as many nervous breakdowns (one after each baby). Wit was supposed to be brilliant and biting, and sometimes was. Records were all pre-1750, the atmosphere rarified and slightly collegiate. There were many paperback books *about* things. Betty's house was a good vacation, a reminder of how the rest of the world lived and thought, and afterwards we would trot gratefully home to our freezing, empty barn of an apartment, our silly, unintellectual conversation, and our lentil soup.

By mid-November it was too cold for any of us to preserve the slightest desire for privacy or solitude. We opened the studio couch to its full width and pulled it in front of the fire, and all took to tumbling into it together at night. The studio couch had a crack down its middle, which seriously limited the gradations and subtlety of physical contact possible between us. That, and the crowding. Usually four of us would be in bed, and one would stay up and keep the fire going: the wood scraps which we got for free didn't burn very long, and there was no way to "bank" a fire and have it burn all night. It was a good feeling to settle down for the night with a full wood box and a book, keeping watch while the rest of the "family" slept snug and content. On warmer nights, when we could afford to let the fire go out and make do with the heat of the oven, four rooms away, the fifth one of us would climb into the slatted bed in the middle room and go to sleep luxuriously alone.

A NIGHT BY THE FIRE: WHAT YOU WOULD LIKE TO HEAR

Maybe I would feel a hand in my cunt, and turn towards its owner, and in doing so I would brush against whomever was sleeping on the other side of me, and feel a hard-on against my hip in passing, and wriggle closer, opening my thighs and closing them around a prick, Leslie's I figure, and put my hand down between my legs to touch its tip with my fingers. The hand in my cunt is Don's and he is turned half away twisted at the waist and is kissing O'Reilley. I come down on it harder, to get it further in, and let Leslie's cock slide out from between my legs and poke around gently in the crack of my ass. I am biting Don on the back of the neck, looking over his shoulder at Pete who is dozing by the fire. O'Reilley throws a leg over Don's hips and I begin to stroke her ankle with my toes. It is slim and smooth and her toes curl up and tickle the sole of my foot, just below the arch. I put my left hand on Don's balls, curl my thumb and index finger around the base of his cock; my thumbnail touches O'Reilley's hand which is just above mine on Don's member. Our hands move in unison. Don's back is beginning to arch, his hand in me is moving swiftly. A tease. I reach behind and under my back with my right hand and make swirls of the hair around Leslie's navel, sliding my fingers over his stomach and down into his bush.

My teeth sink into Don's shoulder. He begins to jump a little. His mouth slides from O'Reilley's lips to her breast, throwing the covers down slightly. The cold air is a shock, but it feels good. I slide my right leg under Leslie and lie with my cunt wide open, pushing against Don's hand. He slows down, and moves in and out of my hole with long strokes. I feel Leslie's pecker jumping against my hip. I let go of Don's balls and take it in both my hands. A large log falls in the fireplace, and Pete wakes up. He takes in the scene and pokes the fire a bit. Leslie slips out of my hands and slides up on the bed, curling around on the top of the pillow above us. I take his dick in my mouth. I hear O'Reilley moaning and realize that Don is on top of her, she is folded nearly double, they are both completely out of the covers by this time. I admire her anemic green color and Don's café-au-lait skin, their long slimness, without breaking the rhythm with which I am sucking off Leslie. Don's hand is still in me, and as he rides O'Reilley he reaches over and kisses me on the mouth. We all four are moving in one rhythm, the bedspring is grooving with it. Don's hand slides out of me, and something else slides in. It is Pete's cock, I decide. I recognize the smell of his hair oil. He has shed pants and shoes and is lying on me in his shirt. I let Leslie's dick slip out of my mouth and start kissing Pete. The bed is crowded; I turn onto my side, turning Pete with me, tucking my knee up into his armpit. Leslie had been kissing O'Reilley's eyelids, now he slips back down on the outside edge of the bed, sliding his wet cock along my side.

O'Reilley and Don nearly fall out of bed, and they move on down closer to our feet where there is more room. I hear Don's sex sounds, reticent growls, and they really turn me on. I feel something poking around with my ass and it is Leslie. I have my back to him. I take my knee out from under Pete's armpit and stretch my leg over his shoulder to give Leslie more room to work, and feel his hands open my ass and his long cock work its way in. I picture the two cocks, Pete's and Leslie's, rubbing against each other through the thin flesh wall inside me. Brothers. Far out. A Good Night.

Maybe we all come once and then maybe Pete sucks Leslie off, Leslie goes down on O'Reilley, while Don and I watch. I guess then Pete would build up the fire, and we would smoke some hash. The wind comes up, it gets much colder, O'Reilley and Pete curl up around each other and go to sleep in the covers. Don starts nuzzling my neck, and we fuck dog-fashion, and Leslie comes up behind Don and slips it in, and we set up some kind of crazy syncopated rhythm that gets the bed rocking again, and Pete and O'Reilley sleep on. Finally we all go to sleep, just before dawn, with one numb arm each stuck under somebody else, and Don's feet stick out of the covers because he's too long. Maybe Silver and Daddi-O, our house cats, come and sit on his feet to warm them and purr through our dreams.

A NIGHT BY THE FIRE: WHAT ACTUALLY HAPPENED

Or maybe not. Pete is poking the fire, and the cheap old phonograph is playing the same Stan Getz record over and over. Don is sitting on the edge of the bed, playing drums with the poker against the fireplace. O'Reilley is lying next to the fire reading Kropotkin's *Appeal to the Young*. The fingers of her left hand play idly with Don's back under his shirt but he doesn't notice. Leslie is lying next to her, flat out on his back, smoking and looking at the ceiling. He has had two dance classes and is exhausted. I am on the cold side of the bed, away from the fire, but I have made up for it by going to bed in sweatpants and sweatshirt. I have a wool cap pulled down over my crew-cut and the covers up to my chin and only my nose and the lower part of my eyes are showing. I am rapping at Pete through the blankets about the surrealists. He grunts whenever I stop but probably doesn't hear anything at all. He is painting. Leslie hands me his cigarette to put out and I put it out on the floor. He says "Goodnight," and turns on his side, his back to me. He has a beautiful body, but his obvious indifference leaves him unattractive and me bored. O'Reilley has finished reading Kropotkin and puts it down on the floor by her side of the bed. "What a shame," she says about nothing special. Don stops drumming and stands up. "I'm going out," he says. "I'll be back in a while." He bends and kisses O'Reilley on the forehead, mumbles, "Good-bye, Baby," and splits. Pete fixes the fire and starts drawing a picture of the three of us going to sleep. We are curled up, spoon fashion, all on our right sides, facing the fire. My nose is cold. My nose is always cold, and usually numb. I stick it deliberately into Leslie's back to warm it. He jumps a little, in his sleep.

* * *

All this while we were poor and getting poorer. There was a stretch of several months when we all four lived on sixty dollars a month, which I earned modeling. The rent was thirty-three dollars, and the lights and gas came to about seven or eight, so that left us about five dollars a week for food. We ate oatmeal a lot, and kidney beans or lentils with rice at night, and sometimes we had eggs for lunch, which we could get in the markets on Ninth Avenue for twenty-nine cents a dozen. Bacon ends and chicken gizzards were nineteen cents a pound. People came to dinner a lot, always at least two or three of them, and they knew that they should bring bread or firewood. They would arrive with stolen loaves, stale loaves, fresh, newly baked and bought French bread, whatever they could lay their hands on, and it would augment the bean soup and make it into a meal. Sometimes they brought wine. Or they would arrive, bundled up to the ears, with wood in tow: great six-by-six beams from old houses, doors, discarded furniture, which they would proceed to saw up in the living room, cursing and groaning, while the soup cooked.

"They" would be Big John, who was an Ayn Rand addict, and Painter John, who was the youngest of us, sixteen at the time and, everybody said, a genius (though nothing ever came of it), and various dancer friends of Leslie's—tough little girls and fragile boys from Ballet Theatre with bags of rolls—and various actor friends of Pete's dropping in after an event at the Studio and stalking about the front room in their trenchcoats, bringing their conglomerate and heavy presences to bear wherever they paused. They often had money, and would bring cake and ice cream and other incongruous goodies; and it was their style that led us to coin the often-used phrase "Do it for the Studio"—applied whenever a situation or individual became ponderously dramatic and self-important.

There was, too, a great miscellany of people that Susan and I had collected: Noah, a Bowery bum and eurhythmics expert, who would hold forth on the shattering beauty of sharing a studio in the nineteen-thirties—or was it the twenties?—with Malvina Hoffman, while his long, red, chapped hands fluttered in the air and his ragged coat flew open and flapped around him; and dykes who were plumbers or printers; and young jazzboys; and sad Bohemian longshoremen; and various Poundians we had discovered in bookstores. We would eat and talk and plan enormous projects in which all the arts would be combined and the programs written in Chinese. Everyone would get a little stoned, and then we would all go out and romp in Central Park, or go down to the pier and look at the river.

When we wanted extra money for luxuries—dry cleaning, or a meal out so that we wouldn't feel too pushed—we would sell some books. Nearly everyone in the house had something going with the book clubs, especially the art book clubs that were flourishing at that time. Books arrived for us under all kinds of names, all over the city, and we duly sold them for a third of their list price, or traded them at Doubleday's for presents for each other.

But finally in January it got really cold; for a while it was just too cold to sleep in the house, five below zero for a few days, I remember, and we all abandoned ship temporarily. Leslie gave up first, and went back to live with his parents in upstate New York. Then Pete, who had been flitting in and out of the scene anyway, took a (heated) furnished room a couple of blocks closer to the League with Big John, who had decided to become a painter in the best *Fountainhead* tradition. Don acquired the use of a Central Park South apartment, whose sad, gay owner was on a winter cruise. And O'Reilley and I took a job and moved into it.

The job was in the tiny West Forties apartment of a public relations man named Ray Clarke. I wasn't ever sure exactly what he did, or what it was that we did for him. I only had the unformulated certainty that we were being used—by whom and for what nefarious purpose I could never determine. The only other person who ever gave me that feeling was Timothy Leary and that was years later.

Ray lived in the bedroom of the apartment, in a great welter of files and tape machines. The bedroom was his sanctuary, his inner office. Here he lived in a maroon smoking jacket and slippers, and drank and smoked lots of cigars and did small black magics. Hardly noticeable, they changed almost nothing, but they kept the air around him moving, and they kept him rich.

The living room of the place had a bar and a sunken goldfish pond, an enormous couch and two desks. It was there that Susan and I plied our labors. She mixed martinis. I typed small numbers of letters and answered the phone. We both got sent out for food, or cheesecake from the Turf at two a.m. We came to work at eleven at night and worked through the early morning, usually quitting sometime between seven and nine and falling out on the couch or the rug.

Every night around eleven, which was just about when the shows let out, a stream of visitors would start flowing into Ray's living room: models, and gangsters, and would-be actors, call girls, gamblers, men from the clothing business, movie stars, composers, and publicity people. Everyone wanted something. There were people pursuing broads, by-lines, money, dope, parts, jewels, supper. Guys who talked legs, and guys who talked breasts, and guys who talked other guys. Girls with little dogs and big backsides, madames, and guys who sold questionable stock. They drank and talked and waited for the one with the role, the one with the magazine, the one with the chow mein. They were mean and ruthless and lecherous, and they thought of themselves as sentimental and sincere. They bought Susan and me three suppers a night because we sat there with holes in our sneakers and grinned.

Ray was supposed to be an expert on getting your name in the columns of the local papers. In reality he was an expert on getting the big stars who were his clients to do what he wanted them to do, which was usually something that would make one of his clients—who *wasn't* a big star yet—famous. The unknown paid Ray a whole lot of money. The big star didn't say no because Ray had too much unsavory information to release to the newspapers—information which he had mostly gleaned from his intercom system (always turned on) as he sat in his inner office, often with a wire recorder turned on beside it.

Ray was always taking everything he could find off my desk: papers, poems, the books I was reading. I would have to go into his bedroom and steal it all back. He had a file in which he kept, alphabetically by author, every personal letter, postcard or photo he had ever received, plus quips and quotes of the various souls who wandered through.

"Honey," he would say, "you wanna be in Earl Wilson's column as the girl who went to visit Ezra Pound?"

"No thanks, Ray," I would say, "I don't think it's a good idea."

"OK, honey, it's your life, but you really need some publicity. Everybody needs publicity."

I learned a lot from Ray.

Learned to assume that everything was tapped; to get up and whisper if I had anything really interesting to say to anyone in a strange apartment. Learned not to leave pieces of paper lying around. Learned not to drink much with strangers, and never to trust theatre people. Pocketed innumerable taxi fares and took subways. Got smuggled in through the back doors of countless expensive restaurants because the people who were taking us out to dinner couldn't—or were ashamed to—bring us in through the front.

Ray was also into some strange and unholy racket having to do with storm windows, but just what the scam was I never did figure out. All I knew was that the personnel on that one was *really* unsavory: scowling and unfriendly, with probably shoulder holsters.

So Susan and I sat there and answered Ray's mail, and took strange tapes to detective agencies, and delivered mysterious bundles of papers in Queens through a taxi window, and met Marlon Brando, who looked bugged and sad, and was. All the time we were there he was being pursued by a noisy brunette named Margie who he had dated once on orders: all in the game. Margie was one of Ray's "clients." She was in love with Brando because he had taken her to his hotel and played her *Tosca* all evening instead of trying to make out. And in love with Margie was Morris Kahn, a big, quiet guy in the clothing business. Morris paid Ray to do publicity for Margie; he also bought Susan some shoes and generally looked after us while he told us all about his troubles with his lady, who wanted him to be as "polite" as Brando.

It was all amusing, but it wasn't serious. And after a while it got spooky. Billy Daniels got shot, and for reasons we couldn't quite follow that shook Ray up a lot. Then the little men with the storm windows began to assume threatening attitudes, and took to wearing their hats in the house and leaning on the bar morosely at ten o'clock in the morning—the very time when Susan and I liked to fall out on the big couch and sleep the day away. Ray began to talk about going to Bermuda for a while. We decided it was getting uncool, and it was now mid-February and warmer anyway, so we split and went home.

When we got back we tried one other job. We were supposedly slinging hash on the weekends for an afterhours club in Harlem located in somebody's pad, but we wound up smoking opium with the guys on our first night there, and three days later found ourselves sitting in a large dark basement room watching a TV set with a red filter over the screen and the sound turned off, to the tune of a Sonny Rollins record, while all around us black girls in bright wigs—chartreuse and lavender—lounged on the fat old sofas and ate egg rolls. It was very jolly and friendly, but riding home next day in a taxi down the Westside Highway through a strangely distorted city, watching the cabdriver's head grow larger and smaller, we decided that though the job was a good one it took too much out of us and on Friday night when the guys showed up again to drive us to work, we regretfully told them so.

Chapter 13—
Organs and Orgasms: An Appreciation

In the Spring for a while I found myself the sole occupant of Number Six, Amsterdam Avenue, and it was then and there that I instituted the custom of giving keys to all my lovers; there were at that time six or seven of them. At this time I got a real double-bed mattress and box spring, and I put them under the window in the front room, and we would watch the moonlight fall on the fire-escape and the moon rise over the Miles Shoe factory across the street, and the fire crackling in the fireplace at our feet, and it was good times. Everyone came in differently, everyone took me on a different trip; it was like six mythologies, six different worlds.

There was Georgie Cunningham. Georgie I had met at a jam session in the West Village that Morris Kahn sent me to when I was working for Ray. Morris had been in the habit of going, but wasn't anymore because the girl Margie was taking all his energies, and he thought maybe Susan and I would enjoy the scene.

We went on a Friday night to the address he gave us, which turned out to be a storefront with curtains on the windows, and cots and couches in rows lining the walls. There we met Georgie, who played sax, and was very shy and very smart, and his friend Kip the drummer, sharp and a bit of a con man, and a funny, big, gentle bass player whose ears stuck out and who informed me solemnly that he only played bass for a living, was really a painter—he having made $12.50 playing bass in the last two weeks. We settled in and listened, and ate poisonous local Chinese food out of containers, and slept in odd corners, and it was Monday afternoon before the kids got through blowing. Then we picked ourselves up and scuttled back to Ray's, getting there just in time for a bath and a meal before the usual crowd arrived, thirsty and ravenous as always.

Georgie was the shyest and the youngest of the people there—maybe seventeen—but when he let go with a horn he outstripped everyone, black and white. There was only one person there who could keep up with him, and that was Brenda, the little jazz singer. Brenda was tiny and redheaded and a ball of fire, dressed always to kill in kelly green or bright yellow, and she thought she was Peggy Lee. She was in love with Kip the drummer, and Georgie was a little in love with each of them.

On the third session that I went to, I lay down with Georgie on a dusty couch on a Saturday afternoon, after a full twenty-four hours of music. Lay down with him and unzipped his fly. Georgie was shy and fastidious. He stopped me and led us both into the bathroom, where we stood in the shower under a funky, slow stream of lukewarm water, and soaped ourselves with stolen motel soap slivers, and washed and slipped and slithered, falling soapy against each other, sliding thigh over slippery thigh. And kissed, ears and eyes full of water, and Georgie slowly got hard and large and I went down on him while drying him off on a raunchy bathmat that said "Hotel Marlton." We finished with me bent over the bathtub, and him slapping against me as he held me around the waist.

After that Saturday afternoon, Georgie took to finding his way uptown every week or so, and we would make out together in my big new bed. He wasn't much of a lay as far as technique went, but he had an angelic quality that was really refreshing, left one rejuvenated, feeling very intense and peaceful. His body was slight, the skin of his stomach particularly pleasing: very pale and very smooth, and his stomach totally flat, with slender hips. His cock was not terribly big, was uncircumcised, and curved ever so slightly to the right when extended to its full length. He liked mostly to fuck, was not too much on games, preferred me to be on the bottom, was passionate, but briefly so. Innocent and keen-eyed. He often came before I did, which distressed us both, and he would finish by finger-fucking me. After a while we got better at each other's timing. He would usually enter the house silently, and I would awaken with a vague sense of someone else in the room to find him sitting on the edge of the bed, thoughtfully watching me sleep.

Georgie brought me Antoine. I had invited him to dinner one evening, together with Kip the drummer and Brenda, and arrived back from a modeling job to find not

Georgie or Kip, for they hadn't come yet, but a huge, stalwart-looking, solemn-faced man in tie and jacket sitting incongruously on a construction bench in front of the fire.

"Hello," he intoned with heavy accent. "I am Annntoine."

"Too much," says I, and it was.

"Georrrrge invited me to meet him here for dinner."

"He did, did he?" I muttered. Georgie was getting a bit far out for my taste.

"Just pull out that end of the mattress, will you?" I asked as brightly as possible. "I want to finish making the bed."

Antoine complied with solemn gallantry, inquiring the while, "And what—is yourrrr—philosophy?"

"Catch," I said, and threw a corner of the blanket to him.

He caught it and tucked it in, making really professional hospital corners while he continued, "Mine—is the philosophy—of rrresigned—desperation," as if he had rehearsed it, which I am sure now that he had.

Antoine was truly and actually French, and a writer, he claimed, showing me once after two years' acquaintance a two-line poem: something about salt and snow and a young boy walking through, very white-on-white effect, very French, I remember thinking. He had had a whore for a mother, or at least a lady of very questionable virtue, and, apparently, a Jewish father who was a Communist heavy of some sort in Paris. He had spent his childhood on the streets, living in bombed-out buildings with roving gangs of kids like himself. He had stories to tell in which the oldest of the urchins, a girl of twelve, bullied them, fucked them, and mothered them, cooked and cleaned and sent them out to steal chickens, and, in real emergencies, went out and hustled for them. When he was about seven he was selling dirty pictures to the soldiers. First the German soldiers and then the American ones.

I don't know how Antoine got to America, but he had, when I knew him, an American painter wife with a small but solid reputation, and a part-scholarship to NYU. We all got very fond of him, he had a mordant bitter wit and he came on like a G-man. When there was trouble, as there sometimes was, between us and the neighborhood street gang, I would go out with Antoine to the local hangout, and we would hold hands and drink a soda together, and generally make it known that he was my guy. His size alone was impressive: he was six foot four and weighed about 220 pounds. And his trench coat harked back to forties tough-guy movies.

He usually entered the house with a good bit of fanfare. I was awake as soon as he let himself into the kitchen, where he announced his presence by walking broodingly about. Then he would come into the front room and lie heavily on me while kissing me formally awake. He was good with his lips, as I have noticed Frenchmen are. They are not great cocksmen, being a little smug in that area, but they do tend to have good mouths. Great tongue-in-ear people, neck-nibblers, and cunt-eaters.

Antoine could usually be induced to get out of his clothes, but it wasn't easy: he operated on the principle that anytime, anyway, anywhere was the way to fuck, like on

163

the floor if somebody was crashing in the bed. He was very insulted the time I refused, the kitchen floor being a bit too grungy for me. He expected me to be hot at a moment's notice, and I could usually oblige, for that spring I went to bed expecting someone or something to happen, and the nights when it didn't were fortunately rather rare.

He liked to go down on me, and had a good repertoire of tongue rhythms and twirls. He also liked for me to suck him off. He was very meticulous about how; had a whole routine worked out of the rhythms and pacing he liked best. It was actually a bit like taking an exam. He always asserted that French girls went down on you best, claimed it was cultural—they were trained from the cradle in phallic worship by their mothers.

He was only a fair lay; his girth turned me off—that, and the fact that he almost never took his socks off. His cock was thick but rather short, and although thick cocks are nice, and make you feel good and full, I myself have never found that width made up for length—I like to feel them touch my cervix. Then too, he was inordinately involved with technique: fucking him was rather like a class in acrobatics, with a little hatha yoga thrown in on the side.

But fuck him I did, and fairly often. There was something strangely comforting about him: something solid and manly after all the boys I'd been going to bed with.

Like Don, for instance. He was still on the scene, would come over, silent and long and sad, and slip into bed. Or more often would wake me by whispering that he had a taxi waiting, and why didn't I go with him, back to his pad on Central Park South. And I would get up and scramble into some tattered jeans and we would cab back through the city and slip past the disapproving doorman. He would have put on the electric coffeepot before he left, and the coffee would be ready and the phonograph would still be playing as we walked in. We would wander from room to room over the pale blue wall-to-wall carpet, shedding our clothes. We would switch from coffee to cognac, shower in the dazzling bathroom, rubbing each other down with the thick, deep-colored towels and exotic Indian oils, and wind up on the huge bed in the draperied bedroom.

Don's reticence was mainly verbal; physically he was quite there, an electricity under his pale brown skin that set my blood tingling, though I couldn't have said quite why. It is an interesting question, this question of "sexiness." Shy Don certainly was, and he had a certain awkwardness, but—a big "but" this—he turned me on, literally set my head spinning, and I set this down finally to a charge in the flesh like static electricity, a superabundance of life force (animal magnetism? orgone?)—a something that crackles, palpably, at the touch.

Making it with him was more tantalizing than satisfying. There was a certain sadness in it, a turning and turning away. His cock was really beautiful, long and slender tool, infinitely expressive; his coloring was indescribable; and he had beautiful hair: curling in tight ringlets like a cap all over his head. He was the size and shape I liked best too: a little too long and too thin—an exaggerated, elongated elegance. But none of this was the essence of it. His essence was shadows, and colorless gleams in the dark. Or the flash of his warm skin, golden sheet-lightning. Elusive. A sideways mover with a glint in his eye, looking back at you over his shoulder.

Mornings, Don's and my scene bordered on the incestuous: a certain amiable brother-and-sister quality, Cocteau-like, as we lounged about in simplistic nudity on the large stuffed chairs, reading and sipping orange juice, or watching the early morning news on television in the large curtained living room.

Sometimes the door would open and it would be Ivan, grinning, returned from some exotic city in the center of the country, and ready to leap into bed in the middle of the afternoon. He had married and was back in school, would reek of ivy and crumbling academic walls and the endless dusty breezes off the plains of the Midwest. But not to be believed, his professorial airs, for the old glint was still in his eye, and I no sooner got him out of his tie and gaiters than he was tipping me over on the wine satin quilt and checking out all my reflexes with tongue and tool.

I was always glad to see Ivan because I knew he would fill the bill, big enough to meet all my requirements. A wholly absorbing cock, that left me neither latitude nor thought for anything else. We would romp the daylight away on the totally familiar fields of each other's body, and then go out in the twilight and roam through the city, taking a taxi up the West Side to the north tip of the island, Endwood Park, going down on each other in that damp and chilly wood, while all around the faint rustle of wildlife was the rustle of the gay boys cruising. Then we'd ride the subway to a Chinese restaurant in Harlem, and walk back to Sixtieth Street through Central Park, dodging the cruising police cars (for there was by now a curfew on the parks), crouching together behind boulders and bushes, feeling each other up for the hell of it in our breathless criminal excitement.

We would return to the pad hungry and smoke hash and get hungrier, devour everything in the kitchen—down to Bosco sandwiches on whole wheat toast—and fall into bed sticky with milk and honey to fuck till dawn, our flesh glowing silver and magic in the moonlight that bounced off my fire-escape.

Ivan was always excitement, riches, a certain sparkle in the air. Pete was home, and dumpiness, and Swiss cheese sandwiches on rye bread for lunch. Making it with him was like having crumpets and tea—with a certain vague awareness that the crumpets were communion wafers, but no idea at all what to do about that. We had, after all, shared a bed for some six months or so before we started screwing: had agreed at the beginning of that previous fall not to make it until the first snow. And then the first snow had slipped past us somehow, and it was well into the winter, after my job with Ray Clarke, before we got together.

Sleeping with Pete was like sleeping with a life-size teddy bear: furry and affectionate and stolid. I got to like it. Antoine had to hurt one a little before he was excited, a few scratches on the back or some bites here and there; Georgie had to hurt himself. Don needed mystery and silence and great orderliness all around him before he could let go, and

Ivan throve on a certain sparkle and *élan* that wasn't always easy to come up with. But with Pete things could be exactly as they were: there could indeed be mouldy sandwiches at the foot of the bed, dusty oatmeal for breakfast, turned-off gas and electric. One could be excited or excitable or neither, let one's hair down—even have a bit of dandruff. No great enchantment—a kind of bread-and-butter sex.

Soon after we started making it, Pete moved back into the pad, having fled Big John and his furnished room after a night on which—so he claimed—he had come home and found that his roommate had taken a wet, seven-foot oil painting to bed with him. It was a good and fine thing to have Pete as roommate and available lover, and it didn't cramp my style. He was—or seemed to be—totally unjealous, and if he came home and I was busy with someone else, he'd simply go out for an English muffin and coffee. Or I would get up after he was asleep and slip out with Don or Ivan, coming back before dawn to a bedfellow who hadn't stirred.

The only guy at this time who came from downtown, who really came from the downtown scene, was Dirty John. He brought a certain funkiness with him, a certain down-to-earth ambience: rank odor of old clothes and roach killer.

Dirty John really earned his name: he was known for the infrequency of his baths. In the winter he never bathed at all, never even changed his clothes. When November came he put on a certain dark blue hooded sweatshirt that framed his thin, dark, furtive face and made him look like a ghetto vampire, and took it off again the following April. If spring was early, that is. He had a seven-dollar Timex wristwatch with a wide band and when he went to bed he would take off the watch, and the strap would have left a white mark on his grey-colored arm. Color of ashes, bright ferret eyes peering out of the hood. Lithe, limber body—the body of a good second-story man, and the ability to come six or seven times in as many hours.

Dirty John was good fun, was always full of schemes for getting rich quick. My favorite was his plan to buy up a piece of the Arizona desert on one of those two-lane straightaways that cuts through it, and there incorporate a town, and singlehandedly vote in a fifteen-mile-an-hour speed limit, and enforce it with incredible fines as the folk tore through at night. Not a bad plan, actually; I have since been through several towns in the U.S. which subsist in just that way. Orem City, Utah, for example.

Dirty John seldom came to the house, but when he did it was always a special occasion. I remember several times that year when we went to bed about seven and made love six or seven times before getting up around two in the morning to go out and eat something at Rudley's luncheonette on the park. Then, reinforced with extra sandwiches for later, we would wend our way home and fall to again, falling asleep after it got light.

Dirty John was from the Pittsburgh slums, and he was full of a dark paranoia and hopelessness that I recognized in myself, but had never encountered in anyone else. He was sure it was all going to go wrong, finally. He was probably right. But in bed he was a pleasure, there was a fine understatement in his lovemaking, it came on slow and strong, snuck up on you unawares, so that blue lights as of cocaine were melting in your gut before you were quite aware that anything had started to happen. He didn't hold out and wait for you to court him, like Don did; wasn't dumpily there, a mountain in your kitchen window, like Pete was; didn't come on like a heavy who really KNEW, like Antoine; he was just easy, an easy lover who took you apart when you least expected it. Dirty John was good times, camaraderie and good fucking, a small slim body that fitted mine well, and though he never bathed in the winter he did OK that Spring, 'cause he never smelled bad when we got together, and his cock was always clean—what more can a girl ask?

He left me with a good feeling when he split, because I knew the games I dug were being perpetrated in some other corner of the city, silently and secretly carried on. Like the time he told me about, when after three days of solitude and heavy meditation he had gotten in touch with the flying saucer people. They were just coming in through the window to take him away with them, like he'd asked them to, when, he said, he suddenly realized that he wasn't ready yet, and told them so, and they obligingly split. People like that were rare in the middle-1950s, and I treasured Dirty John—a good friend who would arrive on his stolen motorcycle and walk absolutely silent through the kitchen whenever I thought hard about him: sent out a call.

And so they would come, each of them the same, but all of them different. They would wake me before they got to the door, the presence and strong telepathic head would do it, like Dirty John, or when they put the key in the lock, subtle and self-assertive, like Ivan, or when they walked possessive and heavy about the kitchen, like Antoine, or when they came to bed and kissed me hello, and I would kiss back, saying "Who?"—or kissing would recognize touch or texture: the smell of Pete's musty clothes, or Don's expensive cologne, or half-sense an aura in the dark.

And they would clamber half-clothed, hastily, into bed, or sit on the blankets and talk me awake, or they would have brought up some grass or some wine, and I would watch, tousled and sleepy, while they made a fire. There would be the B-Minor Mass to fuck to, or Bessie Smith, and we would have a moon, and open window breezes off the river, or dank, chilly greyness and rain beating down, bouncing off the windowsill in bright, exploding drops, and it was all good, the core and heart of that time. I thought of it as fucking my comrades, and a year slipped by.

Chapter 14—We Set Out

Meanwhile, in the outside world everything was changing faster and more than we realized. We thought we were doing the same things we'd always done because the changes happened in slow motion, but happen they did, and when we looked out the window again we were someplace else.

We had run through a variety of aesthetic games: little magazines for which we couldn't raise any bread, theatre projects in gigantic lofts which never materialized, a visit by me and Susan to Ezra Pound, who wanted us single-handed to change the nature of the programming on nationwide television. Leslie choreographed and produced his first dance recital; Pete's fantasy paintings became eight feet wide and gloomier; I put together *This Kind of Bird Flies Backward*, my first book of poems, and Pete and Leslie solemnly assured me that it could not be published because no one would understand a word of the street slang. Don wasn't accepted at Actor's Studio and made a movie instead. Most of his friends *were* accepted and stopped coming to see us. Miles Davis moved away from Tenth Avenue; we no longer ran into him at three in the afternoon hailing a taxi in his dark glasses, looking as if he had just gotten up.

We lived through the horror of the 1956 election as we had lived through the horror of the Rosenberg executions and the Hungarian revolution: paranoid, glued to the radio, and talking endlessly of where we could possibly go into exile. Every inch of walls and floor in the apartment was covered with murals and wise sayings: "The unicorns shall inherit the earth." "Sacrifice everything to the clean line." "Think no twisty thoughts." Etc., etc. Wilhelm Reich was in federal prison.

The first fallout terror had finally struck, and a group of people were buying land in Montana to construct a city under a lead dome. In New York, the beginnings of neo-fascist city planning were stirring, and the entire area north of our pad was slated for destruction, to make way for what was to become Lincoln Center. The house next door to us, which had been empty for twenty-eight years, and had functioned as our own private garbage dump for as long as we lived there, was suddenly torn down, leaving a number of bums homeless and scattering thousands of rats—most of them into our walls.

Most of the more outrageous gay bars had been closed, and people cruised Central Park West more cautiously: there were many plainclothes busts. There were more and more drugs available: cocaine and opium, as well as the ubiquitous heroin, but the hallucinogens hadn't hit the scene as yet. The affluent post-Korean-war society was settling down to a grimmer, more long-term ugliness. At that moment, there really seemed to be no way out.

As far as we knew, there was only a small handful of us—perhaps forty or fifty in the city—who knew what we knew: who raced about in Levis and work shirts, made art, smoked dope, dug the new jazz, and spoke a bastardization of the black argot. We surmised that there might be another fifty living in San Francisco, and perhaps a hundred more scattered throughout the country: Chicago, New Orleans, etc., but our isolation was total and impenetrable, and we did not try to communicate with even this small handful of our confreres. Our chief concern was to keep our integrity (much time and energy went into defining the concept of the "sellout") and to keep our cool: a hard, clean edge and definition in the midst of the terrifying indifference and sentimentality around us—"media mush." We looked to each other for comfort, for praise, for love, and shut out the rest of the world.

Then one evening—it was an evening like many others, there were some twelve or fourteen people eating supper, including Pete and Don and some Studio people, Betty McPeters and her entourage, people were milling about, drinking wine, talking emphatically in small groups while Beatrice Harmon and I were getting the meal together—the priestly ex-book-thief arrived and thrust a small black and white book into my hand, saying, "I think this might interest you." I took it and flipped it open idly, still intent on dishing out beef stew, and found myself in the middle of *Howl* by Allen Ginsberg. Put down the ladle and turned to the beginning and was caught up immediately in that sad, powerful opening: "I saw the best minds of my generation destroyed by madness . . . "

I was too turned on to concern myself with the stew. I handed it over to Beatrice and, without even thanking Bradley, walked out the front door with his new book. Walked the few blocks to the pier on Sixtieth Street and sat down by the Hudson River to read and to come to terms with what was happening. The phrase "breaking ground" kept coming into my head. I knew that this Allen Ginsberg, whoever he was, had broken ground for all of us—all few hundreds of us—simply by getting this published. I had no idea yet what that meant, how far it would take us.

The poem put a certain heaviness in me, too. It followed that if there was one Allen there must be more, other people besides my few buddies writing what they spoke, what they heard, living, however obscurely and shamefully, what they knew, hiding out here and there as we were—and now, suddenly, about to speak out. For I sensed that Allen was only, could only be, the vanguard of a much larger thing. All the people who, like me, had hidden and skulked, writing down what they knew for a small handful of friends— and even those friends claiming it "couldn't be published"—waiting with only a slight bitterness for the thing to end, for man's era to draw to a close in a blaze of radiation—all these would now step forward and say their piece. Not many would hear them, but they would, finally, hear each other. I was about to meet my brothers and sisters.

We had come of age. I was frightened and a little sad. I already clung instinctively to the easy, unself-conscious

Bohemianism we had maintained at the pad, our unspoken sense that we were alone in a strange world, a sense that kept us proud and bound to each other. But for the moment regret for what we might be losing was buried under a sweeping sense of exhilaration, of glee; someone was speaking for all of us, and the poem was good. I was high and delighted. I made my way back to the house and to supper, and we read *Howl* together, I read it aloud to everyone. A new era had begun.

Meanwhile the changes started going down around us thicker and heavier than ever—so that even we couldn't help noticing them. The first thing I noticed, and it gave me quite a jolt, was that the pad was going away, was quite used up. Nothing in particular happened, but it just began to have that air about it, that feeling when you unlocked the door and walked in, of a place that hadn't been lived in for some time, where the air had not been stirred. Places do that, I've noticed. They turn round without warning, turn in on themselves, and suddenly it's like living in a morgue, or a refrigerator; the vital impulse that made a hearth, a living center of some sort, has changed directions like an ocean current, and that particular island is no longer in its path. You can tell because even in the height of summer there's a chill in the air, a something that gets into your bones.

The rats were part of it. They had moved in, *en masse*, from the demolished building next door, and they scampered and played about the kitchen at night, making quite a racket. They came in through a hole under the kitchen sink, and we covered it again and again with pieces of tin, till finally there was nothing left to nail the tin to but more tin, and I gave up. But it did often give me a deep shudder as of awe to awaken in the morning and find that a whole loaf of bread in its plastic bag had been carried halfway across the room, or to find, half an inch long, the neat little claw prints of one of my furry roommates in the congealed fat of yesterday's roast.

O'Reilley had already split with our scene more or less completely. Occasionally she did stop down for a night or two, like gingerly putting one toe into some rather scummy water, and then withdrew to the safety and order of her new East Side flat. Don, having completed his movie, decided to take himself seriously and set out for Hollywood. And Pete fell ill, as I have since learned that he does every three or four years: fell seriously, heavily ill with pneumonia and had to be shipped home to Kew Garden Hills in a taxi at his father's expense while his fever raged. The disease itself abated rather quickly, but the weakness remained, and Pete stayed in the comparative luxury of his family's house, eating minute steaks and resting.

It may have been our large rat population that drove Leslie out into the world, but I think it was simply growing pains: he suddenly felt old enough to have a pad of his own, and he set out to get one. He found a loft on Prince Street in a part of the Village that had just opened up. The loft was the top floor of three. They were open to each other at staircase and hall, and they all shared one john. Previous tenants had installed a bathtub and hot water heater on the second floor and Leslie's present downstairs neighbor had just added a small washbasin which also served for everyone's dishes. Leslie had a two-burner hotplate on top of a small, rickety office frig, and a table with three wobbly chairs. All the water came from downstairs and was carted up in gallon wine jugs. It was dumped out the window when one didn't feel like making the trip down to the second-floor john. No one worried about sprinkler systems, exits, or other such regulations; living in lofts was illegal, and everyone who could afford it did it.

The light and space in Leslie's place was lovely: huge front room like a big barn, green plants everywhere. White curtains that were probably just sheets let in the play of light. Almost equally large back room faced north on paved courtyard and endless possibilities of rooftops. And kitchen off to one side. It was the most luxurious (and most expensive) apartment that any of us had attempted yet. It cost eighty dollars a month and we all admired Leslie for braving such a rent.

With the pad, Leslie took on a roommate, a long, lanky funny-looking boy named Benny Hudson. Benny's ears stuck out, and he had a herringbone coat. He smelled of soap and earnestness and other Midwestern virtues, but he had a job and could pay half of the rent—all of it in emergencies—so here he was. He and Leslie were lovers, of sorts. That is, they were making it, and Benny was in love.

As for me, I still clung, out of sentiment and attachment, to the uptown pad. It was my home base, though I slept there seldom now. I had stopped paying rent several months before, but hung on, muttering "Health

Department" at the landlord, whenever he muttered "Eviction" at me. We were at an impasse.

Since I wasn't paying any more rent, the landlord wasn't making any more repairs, which meant that when the local gang broke the windows they stayed broken, and finally nearly all of them were. The place was breezy, but it was getting warm again, and so it didn't matter. Then the lights and gas went off; I took to eating out, eating and bathing in other people's houses, and reading by candlelight, which was scary because of the rats. I didn't relish the thought of meeting a rat as big as a cat by candlelight in my kitchen. I began to look for someplace else to live.

About this time I decided that I wanted to have a baby. It was nothing that I decided with my head, just a vague stirring and impulse in my body, some will to flower, to come to fruition—and something in my cells whispering that the scene as I knew it had gone on long enough, that there were many other states of being to explore. I didn't do anything about it, continued to use a diaphragm when screwing, it was just that my head was in a different place. I began to see everyone as a prospective father, and I found that many people looked ridiculous in this light.

I had been in sporadic correspondence with Allen Ginsberg and some of his friends ever since I read *Howl* (Lawrence Ferlinghetti had even written a tiny introduction for my "unpublishable" first book). Now Allen and his gang were in New York and I was eager to meet them. After a few phone calls back and forth they came down to Leslie's, where I was staying, bringing with them a great quantity of cheap wine and some very good grass. We all proceeded to get thoroughly stoned, and Allen and Jack Kerouac, who was with him, rapped down a long, beautiful high-flown rap all about poetry and high endeavor. Jack's belief, which Allen shared at the time, was that one should never change or rewrite anything. He felt that the initial flash of the turned-on mind was best, in life as well as in poetry, and I could see that he probably really lived that way. He seized upon my notebooks and proceeded to uncorrect the poems, rolling the original bumpy lines off his tongue, making the stops and awkwardnesses beautiful while we all got higher and higher.

I proposed that they spend the night. Allen had eyes for Leslie and agreed readily, enlisting his lover Peter's help in moving the couch from the front room to the back, and setting it beside the double bed. They were about the same height and made one extra-wide, only slightly bumpy, sleeping place. They dragged the whole thing into the center of the room, arranging plants around it, and burning sticks of Indian incense which they stuck into the flower pots. Benny watched, horrified.

After kissing us all lingeringly, Peter split—to what mysterious night rituals of his own, we could only surmise. Leslie lit some candles and placed them at the bedside, turning off the overhead light. Immediately, the room seemed immense, mysterious, the beds an island, a camp in a great forest wilderness (Leslie's rubber plants). We all undressed—Benny with some trepidation—and climbed in.

It was a strange, nondescript kind of orgy. Allen set things going by largely and fully embracing all of us, each in turn and all at once, sliding from body to body in a great wallow of flesh. It was warm and friendly and very unsexy—like being in a bathtub with four other people. To make matters worse, I had my period, and was acutely aware of the little white string of a tampax sticking out of my cunt. I played for a while with the cocks with which I found myself surrounded, planning as soon as I could to get out of the way of the action and go to sleep.

But Jack was straight, and finding himself in a bed with three faggots and me, he wanted some pussy and decided he was going to get it. He began to persuade me to remove the tampax by nuzzling and nudging at my breasts and neck with his handsome head. Meanwhile everyone else was urging me to join in the games. Allen embarked on a long speech on the joys of making it while menstruating: the extra lubrication, the extra excitement due to a change of hormones, animals in heat bleed slightly, etc. Finally, to the cheer of the whole gang, I pulled out the bloody talisman and flung it across the room.

Having done his part to assure a pleasurable evening for Jack and myself, Allen fell to work on the young male bodies beside him, and was soon wrapped round, with Leslie on one side of him and Benny on the other. I head some squeals, and felt much humping and bumping about, but in the welter of bedclothes the action was rather obscure. Jack began by gallantly going down on me to prove that he didn't mind a little blood. He had a wildly nestling, hugging sort of approach, and he was a big man; I was taken over, and lay there with legs spread and eyes closed while he snorted and leaped like Pan. When I shut my eyes I was once more aware of the warm ocean of flesh around me, could distinguish the various love-sounds and breathings of all the creatures.

We finally got loose of the bedclothes: Jack, with a great cry, heaved himself upwards and dumped them all on the floor, then fell heavily on top of me and entered me immediately. My momentary surprise turned to pleasure, and I squirmed down on his cock, getting it all inside of me, feeling good and full. It nudged the neck of my womb, and I felt a thrill of a different kind, a pleasure that, starting in my groin, spread outward to the edge of my skin, stirring every hair follicle on my body separately. We bucked and shifted, looking for the best position, fucked for a long time on our sides. Then Jack withdrew and flipped over on his back. I played with his half-soft cock with the traces of my blood on it, bringing it back to fullness. He indicated by gestures that he wanted me to sit on top of him. I did, guiding his cock inside me, and it touched the same place at the neck of my womb again, but this time more heavily, so that the pleasure was sharper and edged with a slight pain.

It was a long, slow, easy fuck. I knelt with my feet tucked under me and moved up and down on Jack's cock, while his hands on my waist supported and guided my movement. I glanced at the group beside me. Leslie was lying on Allen, kissing him, and they were grinding their stomachs together. I could imagine, though I could not see, their two hard cocks between them, denting the soft skin of their bellies. Benny lay a little to one side of the two of them. He was kissing Leslie's back and neck, and he had his own cock in his hand. Pleasure began to increase in my gut,

I bent down and kissed Jack on the mouth, moving faster and faster against him. His two hands on my shoulders held me warm and tight, as we both came in the friendliness of that huge, candlelit room.

Jack stirred after a few minutes of light rest. He leaned over the side of the bed, feeling around to find his soft leather pouch, and rolled a joint of good Mexican grass. Drew on it deeply and handed it to me. I smoked a little, and looked around to see where the others were at. Allen was lying full out on the bed, and Leslie was fucking him in the ass. I tried to hand the joint to Benny, who refused it with a shake of his head and fell, sobbing, into my arms. I handed the grass back to Jack, and tried to comfort Benny, but he would only lie there, sobbing softly. I stroked his shoulders and back and wished he would stop. It was very boring. Jack caught my eye and grinned at my chagrin. I turned my head towards him and he put the grass back in my mouth, holding it for me while I drew on it. Finally Benny stopped and said, "I have to go to the bathroom." He tromped about with reproachful noises, finding a bathrobe, and was lost in the unfathomed halls and staircases.

Allen and Leslie finished doing their thing, and Leslie was hungry, as he always was after fucking, and went to the kitchen and came back with bread and herring and a bag of early peaches, and he and Jack and I sat munching and smoking, while Allen scribbled in a notebook, occasionally looking up abstractedly for the grass. Jack pulled me between his legs and began to rub his limp cock against my backside and eventually got it hard again, and he exclaimed, "Look, Allen!" and leaped out of bed pulling me onto him as he stood in a deep *plié* and we tried to do it in Tibetan yab-yum position. It felt good, was really fine and lots of fun, but Jack was drunk and high and balance not too good, and we fell over, narrowly missing a plant and went on fucking on the floor, my legs around his waist, while he protested that we should slow down and let him get into lotus position so we could try that one. But I simply locked my ankles around his waist, spread the cheeks of his ass with my hands, kept him busy, and we flipped over first one way and then the other on the floor.

Allen by this time was reciting Whitman and rubbing Leslie's cock with his feet, and when Leslie got hard again he went down on him, and Benny came back from the bathroom and went down on Allen. And then Jack went back into his pouch and came up with a black ping-pong ball of hashish, and we smoked a little and ate the rest, and I fell asleep and dreamed that the aether was flesh and human bodies merely cresting waves upon it. I watched them form and unform all night long.

In the morning I had my period full force, and stayed in bed sitting on a towel while Leslie and Benny pranced out and scored tampax and coffee and eggs from the horrified corner grocer.

And two weeks later, sitting at home in the pad, in a patch of sunlight on the black painted floor, while a small fire blazed for companionship and not for warmth, sitting there in a cloud of plaster dust I had raised by trying to carve a hard chunk of plaster of Paris into the semblance of a hand, white dust in the clean air, the house swept and windy from the broken windows, I heard a key turn in the lock. And turned in white sweatshirt and blue jeans, white plaster dust in my hair, to find Ivan standing in the doorway. Ivan whom I had not seen in many months, who had disappeared into the depths of the South, into some dull southern college where he was teaching. He stood in the doorway, grinning his old grin in spite of necktie and straight overcoat, and stepped—in shiny shoes—across the swept and splintering floorboards, removing professorial gloves.

I put down the half-carved hand and went to greet him: kiss long and fine, though only a small improvement on our kisses of long ago. And we drank brandy together out of coffee cups and ate bread and cheese while he told me about his life, the incredible circuit of "work," of words and money, that had closed around him.

And I, looking him over, seeing how he still moved so fine, sensing the long hard muscles under the straight clothes, the fine bones of the face, high cheekbones that held through the years, good quick mind fumbling now with the foolishness of semantics and logical positivism, bogged down in the karmic round but still shooting sudden sparks, sending magic across the room till we both found ourselves laughing, rolling on the floor with laughter, knees pulled up and brandy spilling—I, noting these good points which were the kernel, and which all the karmic bullshit hadn't changed, flashed for a minute on the possibility that this might be the father I was seeking.

It was the last really fine day in the pad. Ivan as usual

shed his pomposity with his wardrobe, and we fucked all afternoon in the patch of sunlight on the double bed. The quintessence of all the pad had been, the friendly magic and high adventure we had lived in it, all floated around us that afternoon in the dusty air. That life had never seemed more graceful and easy, more filled with kindly love and essential freedom, than it did that day, and I knew I was saying good-bye to it. When Ivan split I lay awake for a long time, staring at the fire-escape and the sparse starlight through the window.

And when the full moon shone on the fire-escape again, I didn't get my period as I should have. And as the moon waned, my breasts grew and became sore, and I knew I was pregnant. And I began to put my books in boxes, and pack up the odds and ends of my life, for a whole new adventure was starting, and I had no idea where it would land me.

Afterword—Writing Memoirs

In March 1968, I did my last theatre piece in New York City. It was called *Monuments*, and was a series of monologues: people played themselves—my take on the insides of their heads. There were eight monologues and any three could be performed in any given order to make a kind of "story," or at least a sequence, and we did them at the Cafe Cino. In the one I wrote for myself I asked if I would ever "sit in a bay window in San Francisco, looking at the rain and writing another novel."

By summer solstice I found myself on a plane with a screaming infant, part of a crew of fourteen "grown-ups" with all their accompanying children, pets, rifles, typewriters, and musical instruments, who were migrating from New York. I had neglected to tell my husband where I was going, as he was in India on our credit cards, and had neglected to leave me any credit, leaving me instead a bevy of beautiful boys he had loved and left (I took two of them along). The crew went west in a variety of ways: planes, and a VW bus (newly purchased with the tag-end of my credit) being the two most notable. I will always remember being met at the airport by the most downtrodden pickup truck I had ever seen, driven by Lenore Kandel, whilst a Digger moppet, age about two, stood beside her in the cab, naked from the waist down and chewing on a hot dog (horrific to my macrobiotic mind). Miscellaneous mutts—mostly canine—shared the back of the truck with us, as we drove into town. My infant refused to stop screaming.

A few months and many horrendous adventures later (*vide* if you will my, like they say, "work in progress" *The California Book*) I found myself ensconced in aforesaid bay window, looking at the heaviest rainy season in ten years, and writing—well, writing for our rent and dinner. Most of the fourteen grown-ups had stayed around, and none of them was working. The one gay woman friend who had the most impressive track record in this regard: ten years in offices in New York, had taken to her bed, to rest and recuperate. And all the other less hardy folk followed suit. Or they were organizing be-ins, delivering free food, selling or manufacturing illegal chemicals, publishing anarchist manifestoes, designing political broadsides, creating lightshows for rock concerts, feeding stray guitarists, or making beaded earrings or candle glasses out of colored pebbles.

In addition, a great bevy of new-found California friends had also moved in, some invited and some not. (We had rented a fourteen-room house with finished basement, in-law apartment, and huge back yard for $300 a month.) I still remember with distinct unfondness the two couples with seven kids between them whom the Diggers installed above my protests on the floor of the dining room. Said couples had just returned from Hawaii where they had gone to "get clean"—get off smack. Diggers who brought them from the airport in my van also brought them a present—more smack. And so they dreamed the time away on my sheepskin scatter rugs. All except one of the men, who was prone to wander the streets in search of hold-up victims, or burn up anything burnable on our altars (wooden statues were his favorite) or clean his guns just behind my back in my study, insisting that if I were *really* a Buddhist it wouldn't bother me, I'd be able to write no matter what he did.

And write I did, and was glad when the S.F. police finally came for him, though I put up the traditional fight: "Do you have a warrant?" etc. Write I did, else how would we all have the seaweed and brown rice and miso soup I deemed necessary for our survival? It was a schizophrenic life. I was sitting zazen every morning at Zen Center on Bush Street, and consequently went to sleep by ten, whilst downstairs people danced in boots on the dining room table, or held war conferences: where to put the children when the shooting starts. I would get up at four, wake the two Michigan zennies on the back porch, and we all three would push the VW van down Oak Street in the pre-dawn light till it started, and drive to Zen Center. On our return, I would make enough oatmeal or rice cream for the army we were, scarf some, and go to my big front room to write before the action started.

I had met Maurice Girodias in New York, and had written the sex scenes for a couple of dull and innocuous novels he had purchased as skeleton plots to which the prurient interest had to be added, like oregano to tomato sauce.

Before I left town he had asked me to write one myself, and when it became obvious that money was scarce, to put it mildly (everything you could possibly want in that San Francisco of 1968—four hundred pounds of free fish, $85 kilos of grass, great cheap wine, free food, beach and sky—everything except cash. Wherever the "prosperity" was, it wasn't where we were)—when, as I was saying, it became obvious that money was scarce, and would likely continue to be so, I got to work, and quickly whipped out enough pages for an advance. It was the first and only time I'd ever written a "potboiler," and it was clearly the course to take.

Money wasn't supposed to be scarce, you understand. Before I left New York, the powers-that-be in Washington had awarded me a $10,000 grant—a considerable sum in those days. It was supposed to arrive in a lump on July 1, a mere ten days after I got to San Francisco. But due to the vagaries of bureaucracy, it didn't even begin to show up till the following January, and then came in small and relatively useless dribbles. Clearly the twenty-odd large and assorted small humans who graced the halls, balconies, and bannisters of my pad had to eat.

And so, I would go from my morning meditation and macrobiotic eats to the typewriter, and sit indeed in the bay window I had requested of the gods, turning out pages of reminiscences, whilst Black and White Panthers, Hell's Angels, parrots, rock bands, assorted Chinese and American Indian dealers and babes without diapers wandered in and out of the room (no one paid attention if you closed the door, and you were asking for trouble if you locked it). As time went on I got more and more into the book, especially the remembering and re-creating of that earlier time, those early fifties in The City. I would play Bird, or Clifford Brown, or Miles' "Walking" over and over as I wrote, and tiny perfect memories of long-forgotten rooms, and scenes, and folks would take me over—which is of course one of the joys of writing prose, and one I was tasting there for the first time. I'm really glad I wrote the book, and wrote it when I did, before the world of the West completely took me: reading it now, there's much that I don't remember, that I read like someone else's story.

Gobs of words would go off to New York whenever the rent was due, come back with "MORE SEX" scrawled across the top page in Maurice's inimitable hand, and I would dream up odd angles of bodies or weird combinations of humans and cram them in and send it off again. Sometimes I'd wander the house looking for folks to check things out with: "Lie down," I'd say, "I want to see if this is possible." And they would, clothed, and we would find out, in a friendly disinterested way, if a particular contortion was viable, and stand up again, completely not turned on, and go about our business.

By noon or one I would have had enough for the day, and close up shop, and wander off to Japantown for raw fish and sake, which I had discovered was the only way to acclimate to the rain and mist and seawind that were a constant on the panhandle. (Eucalyptus trees in fog, the smell of them and dog shit, and the gas fire in the tiled fireplace, is what I remember about those mornings.) After lunch there was play, and beads, and politics, and "real" writing, and all the business and pleasure of those busy days.

And the book got finished, and when the grant came I used it to buy off the husband who had returned from India; and then the scene got heavier and sadder, and the FBI started to show up everyday, and it seemed like time to close up shop and move to the backwoods. All that is another story.

Diane di Prima
San Francisco
Autumn Equinox, 1987

FOR THE BEST IN PAPERBACKS, LOOK FOR THE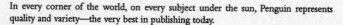

In every corner of the world, on every subject under the sun, Penguin represents quality and variety—the very best in publishing today.

For complete information about books available from Penguin—including Puffins, Penguin Classics, and Arkana—and how to order them, write to us at the appropriate address below. Please note that for copyright reasons the selection of books varies from country to country.

In the United Kingdom: Please write to *Dept. JC, Penguin Books Ltd, FREEPOST, West Drayton, Middlesex UB7 0BR.*

If you have any difficulty in obtaining a title, please send your order with the correct money, plus ten percent for postage and packaging, to *P.O. Box No. 11, West Drayton, Middlesex UB7 0BR*

In the United States: Please write to *Consumer Sales, Penguin USA, P.O. Box 999, Dept. 17109, Bergenfield, New Jersey 07621-0120.* VISA and MasterCard holders call 1-800-253-6476 to order all Penguin titles

In Canada: Please write to *Penguin Books Canada Ltd, 10 Alcorn Avenue, Suite 300, Toronto, Ontario M4V 3B2*

In Australia: Please write to *Penguin Books Australia Ltd, P.O. Box 257, Ringwood, Victoria 3134*

In New Zealand: Please write to *Penguin Books (NZ) Ltd, Private Bag 102902, North Shore Mail Centre, Auckland 10*

In India: Please write to *Penguin Books India Pvt Ltd, 706 Eros Apartments, 56 Nehru Place, New Delhi 110 019*

In the Netherlands: Please write to *Penguin Books Netherlands bv, Postbus 3507, NL-1001 AH Amsterdam*

In Germany: Please write to *Penguin Books Deutschland GmbH, Metzlerstrasse 26, 60594 Frankfurt am Main*

In Spain: Please write to *Penguin Books S.A., Bravo Murillo 19, 1° B, 28015 Madrid*

In Italy: Please write to *Penguin Italia s.r.l., Via Felice Casati 20, I-20124 Milano*

In France: Please write to *Penguin France S.A., 17 rue Lejeune, F–31000 Toulouse*

In Japan: Please write to *Penguin Books Japan, Ishikiribashi Building, 2–5–4, Suido, Bunkyo-ku, Tokyo 112*

In Greece: Please write to *Penguin Hellas Ltd, Dimocritou 3, GR–106 71 Athens*

In South Africa: Please write to *Longman Penguin Southern Africa (Pty) Ltd, Private Bag X08, Bertsham 2013*